Welcome

This coloring book is about having fun. We hope it also encourages you to have a look at medieval manuscripts. Just Google, "Medieval Manuscripts". There are tens of thousands of Manuscripts waiting to be explored.

I want to thank the many great British libraries for making these documents available online.

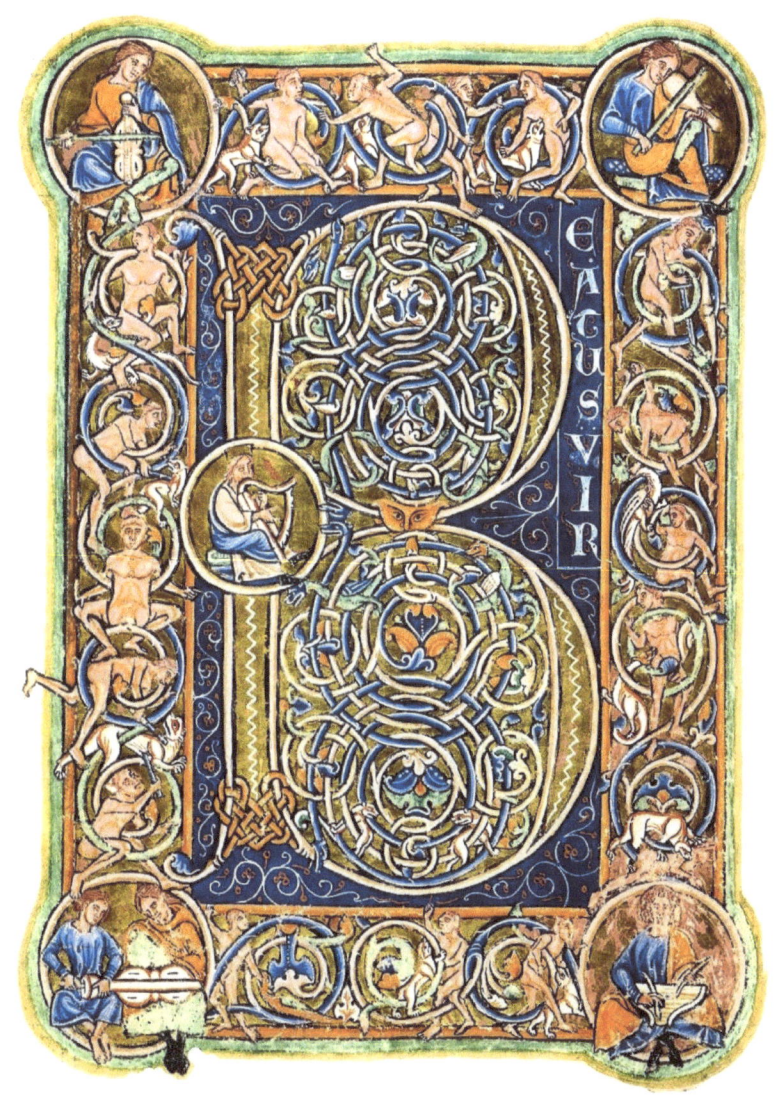

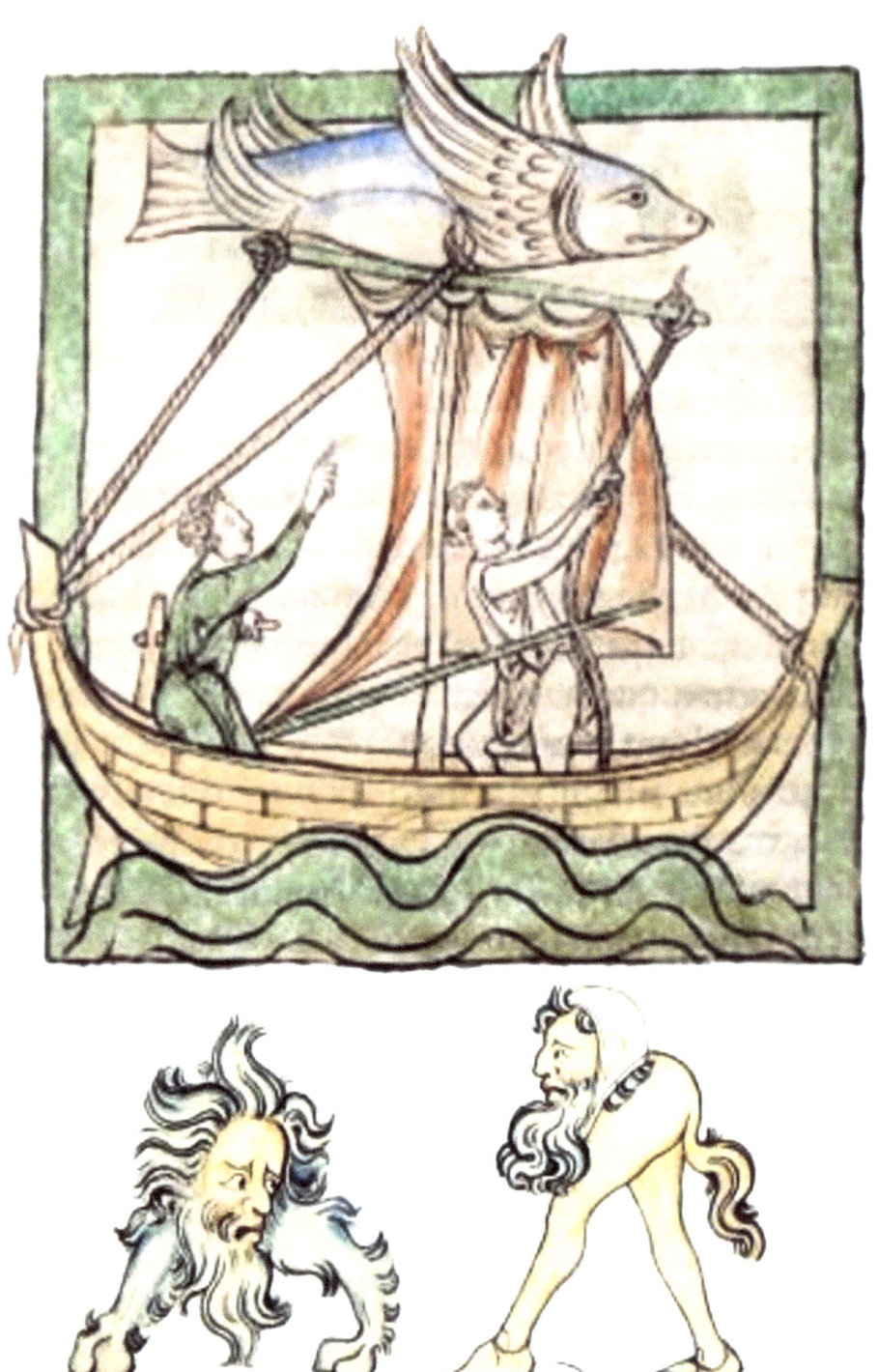

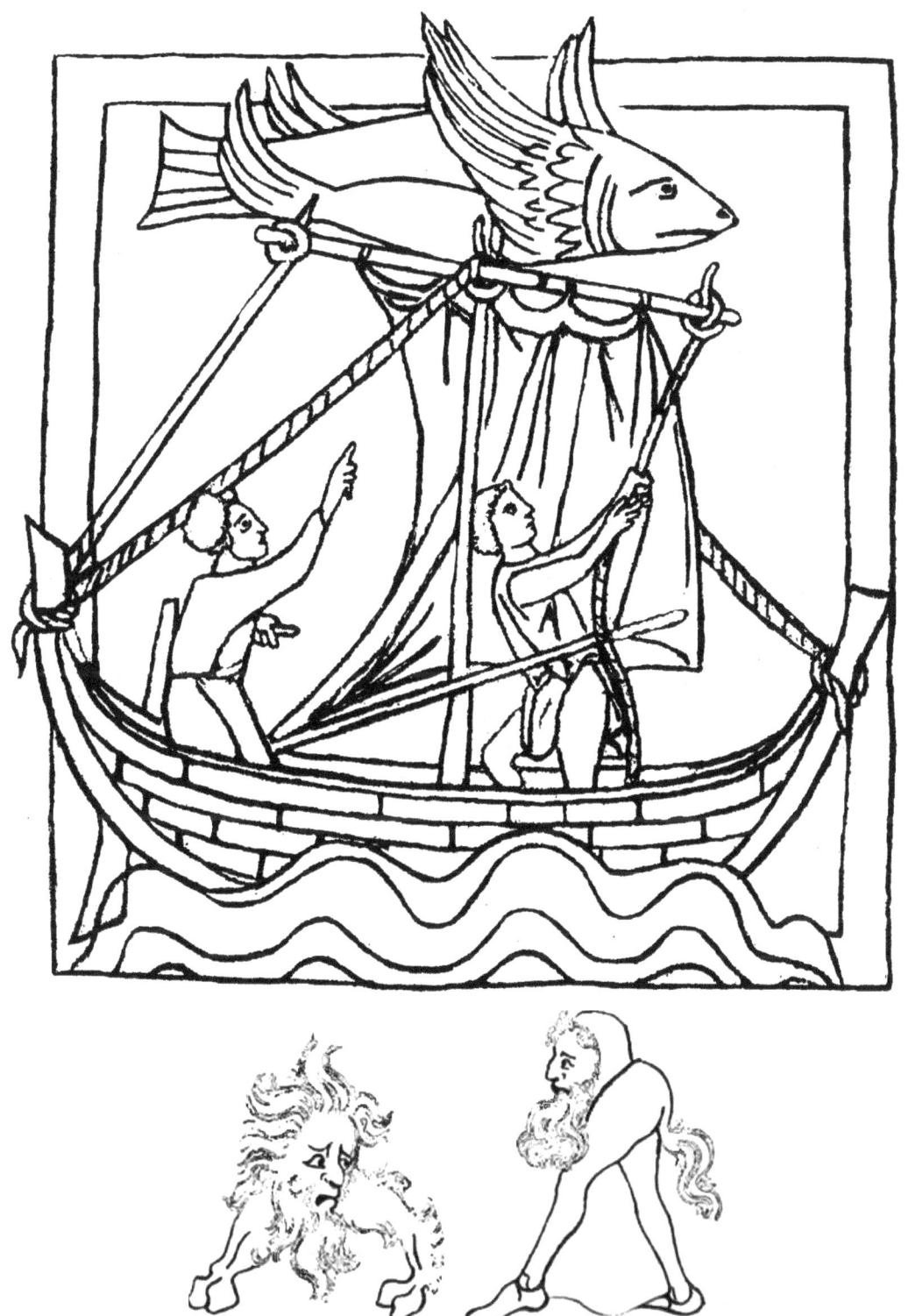

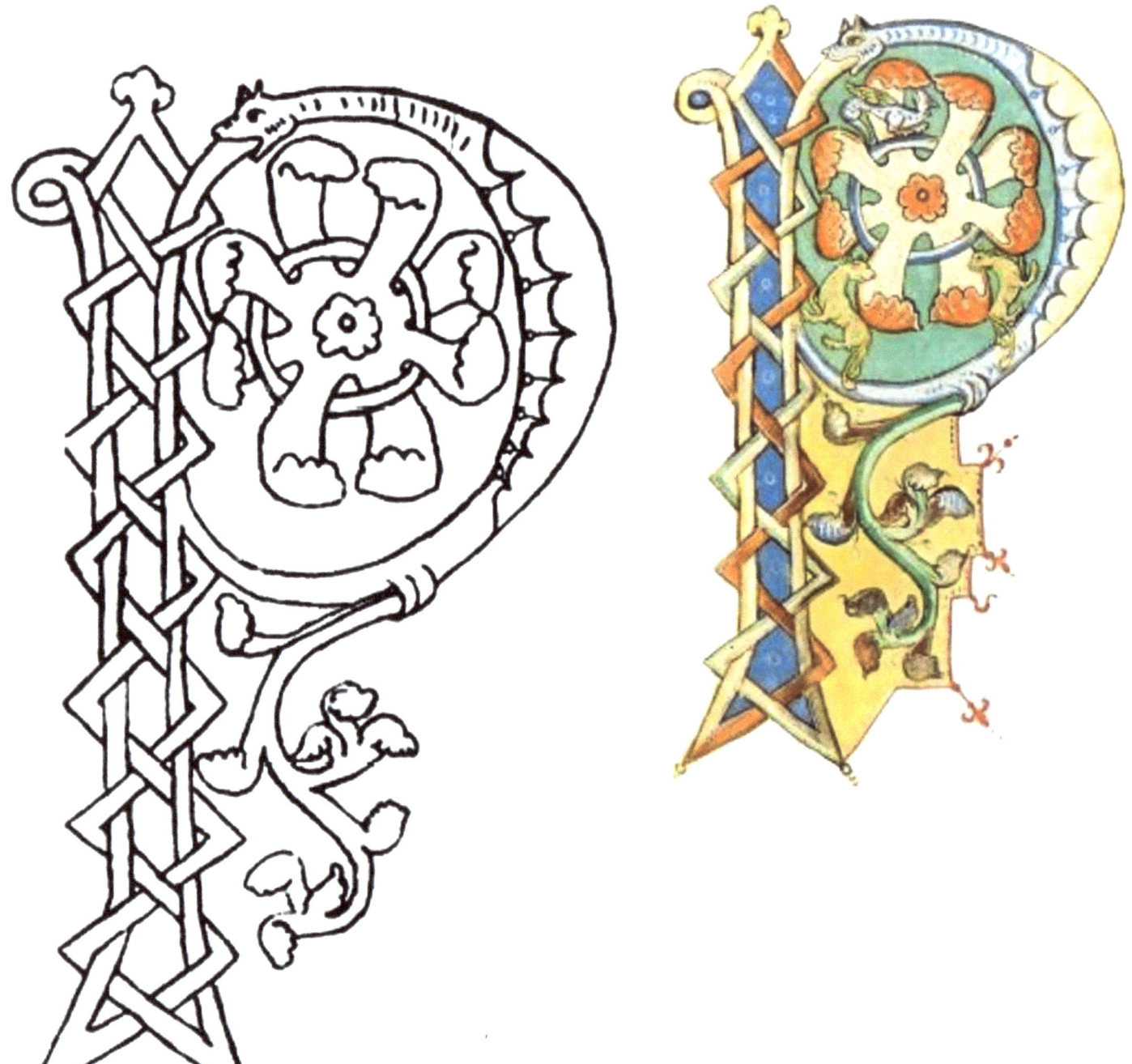

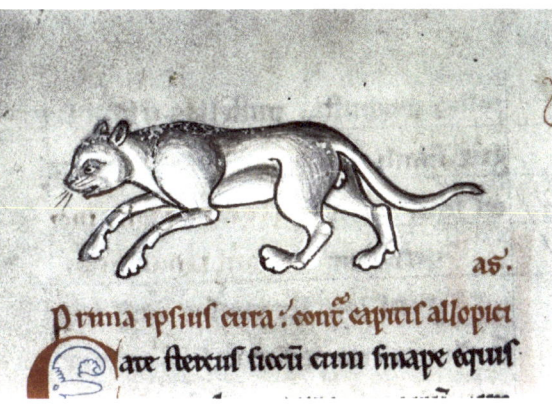

Prima ipsius cura: conf capitis allopici
are flercus ficcu cum finape equis

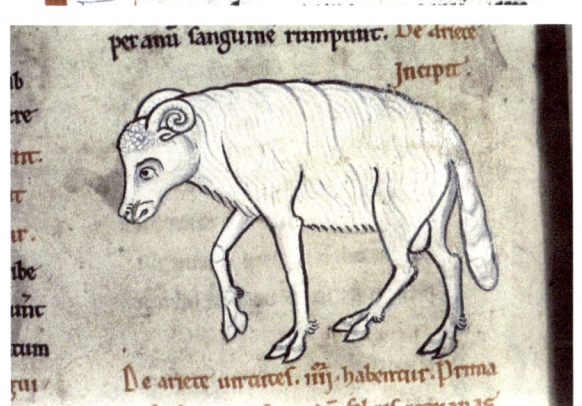

per anu sanguine rumpunt. De ariete
Incipit

De ariete untates. iiij. habentur. Prima

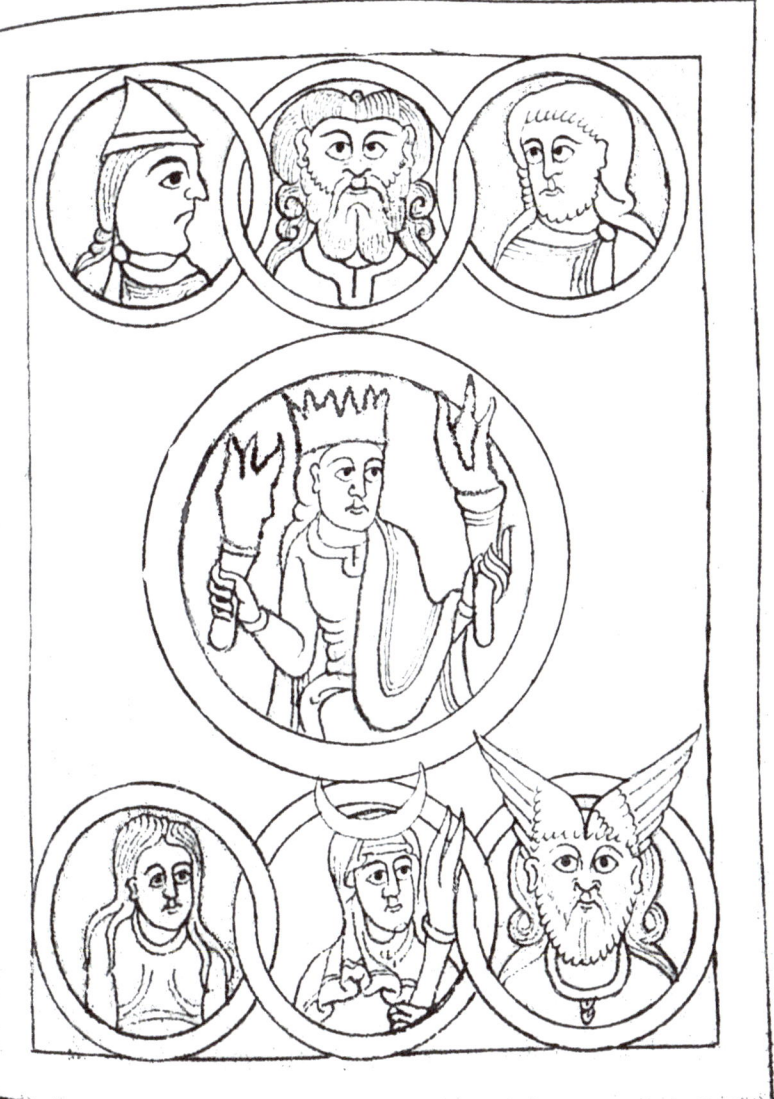

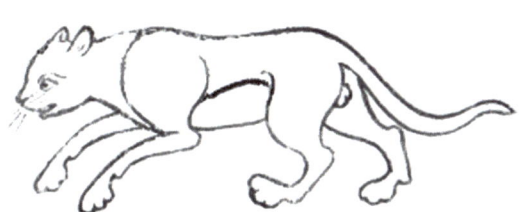

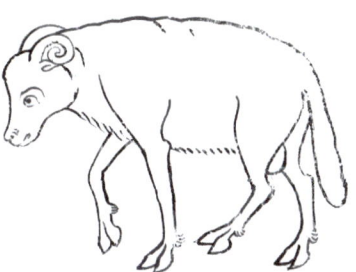

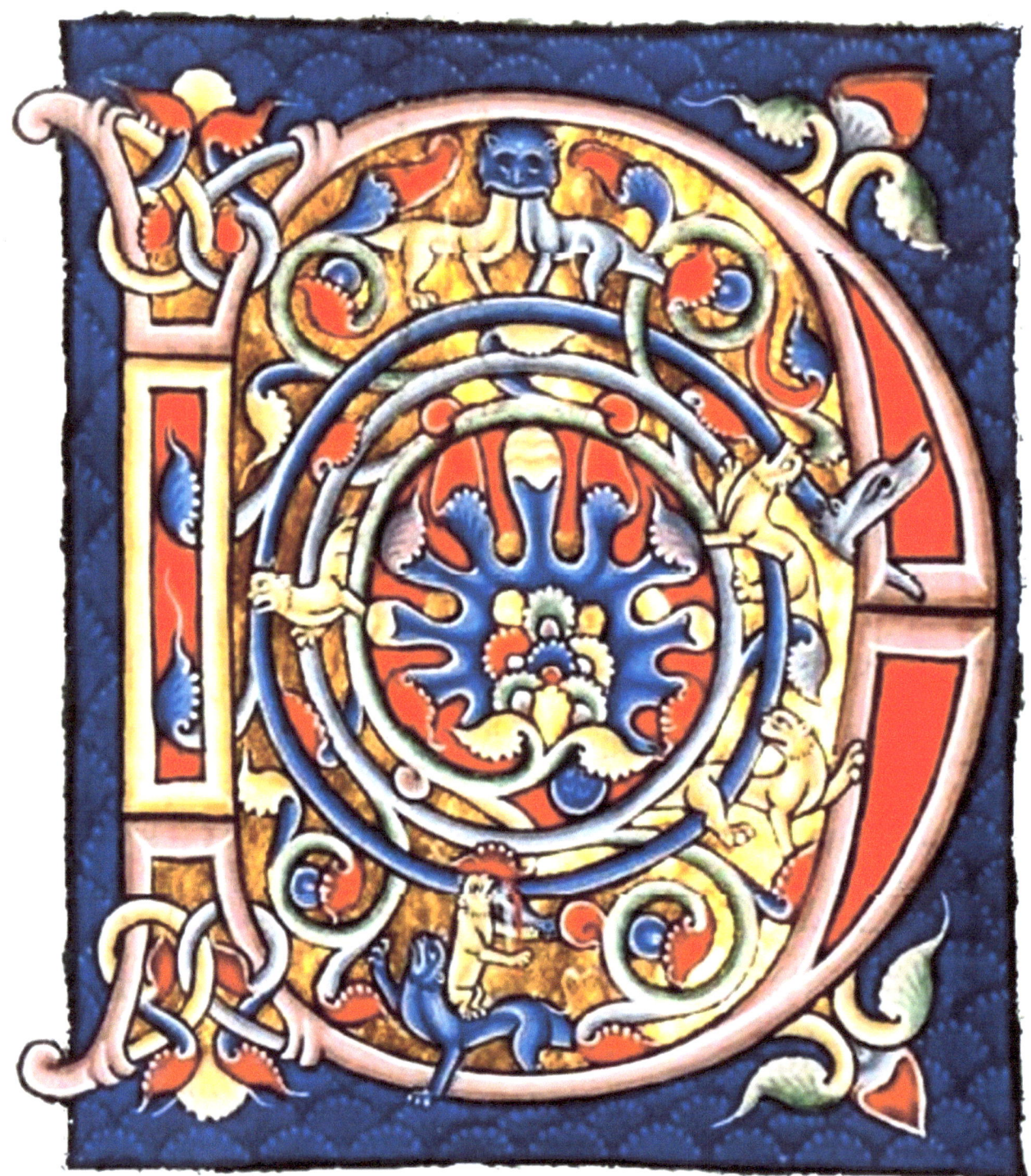

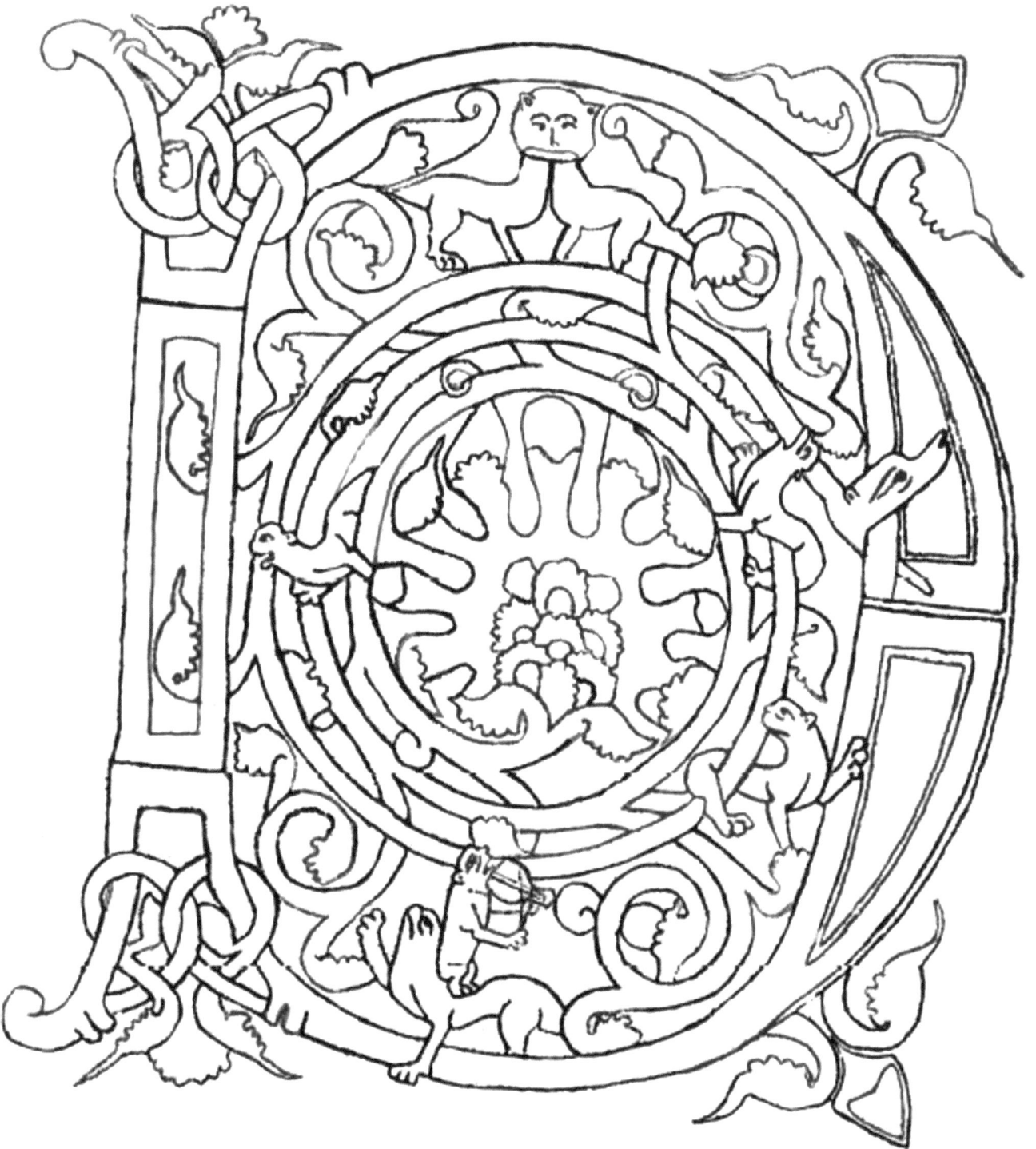

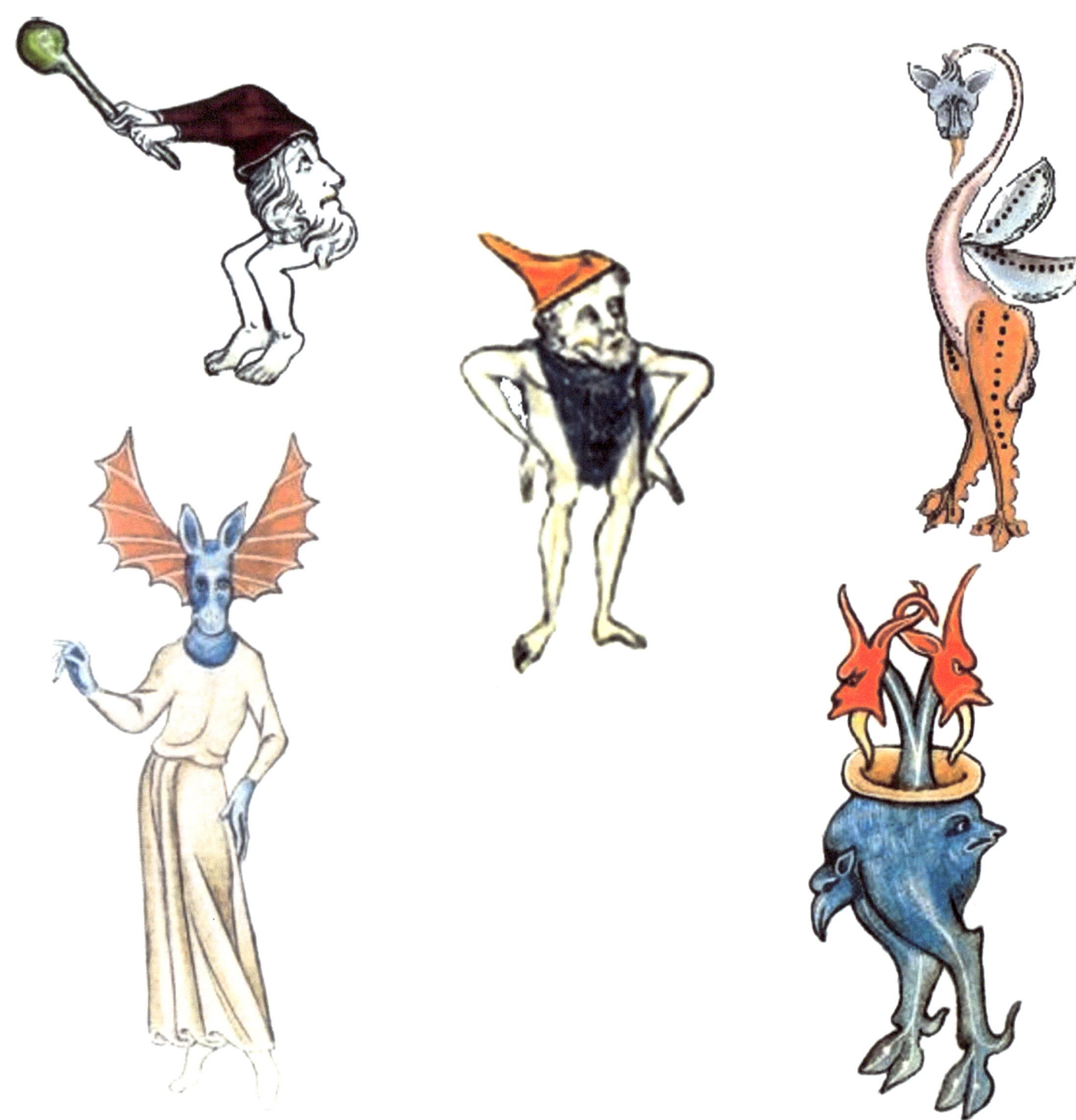

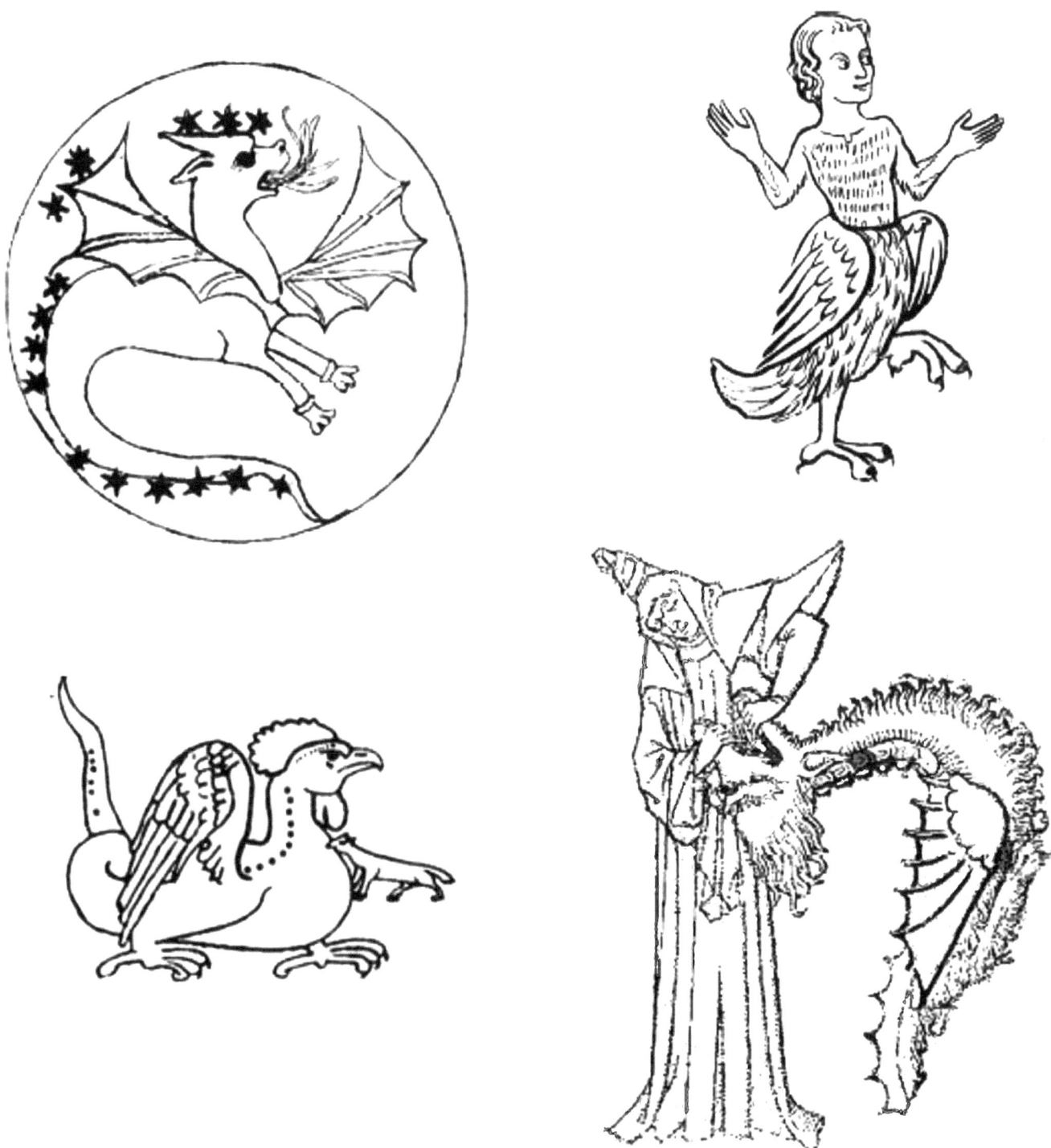

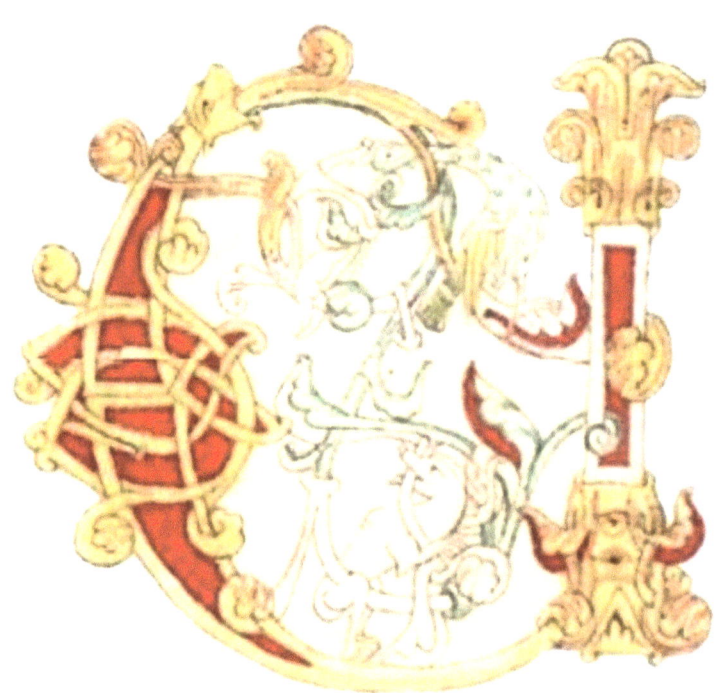

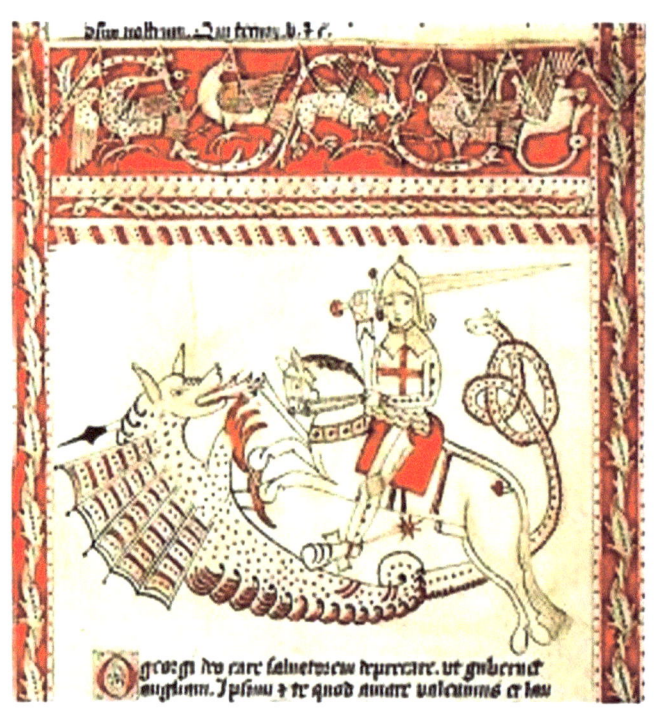

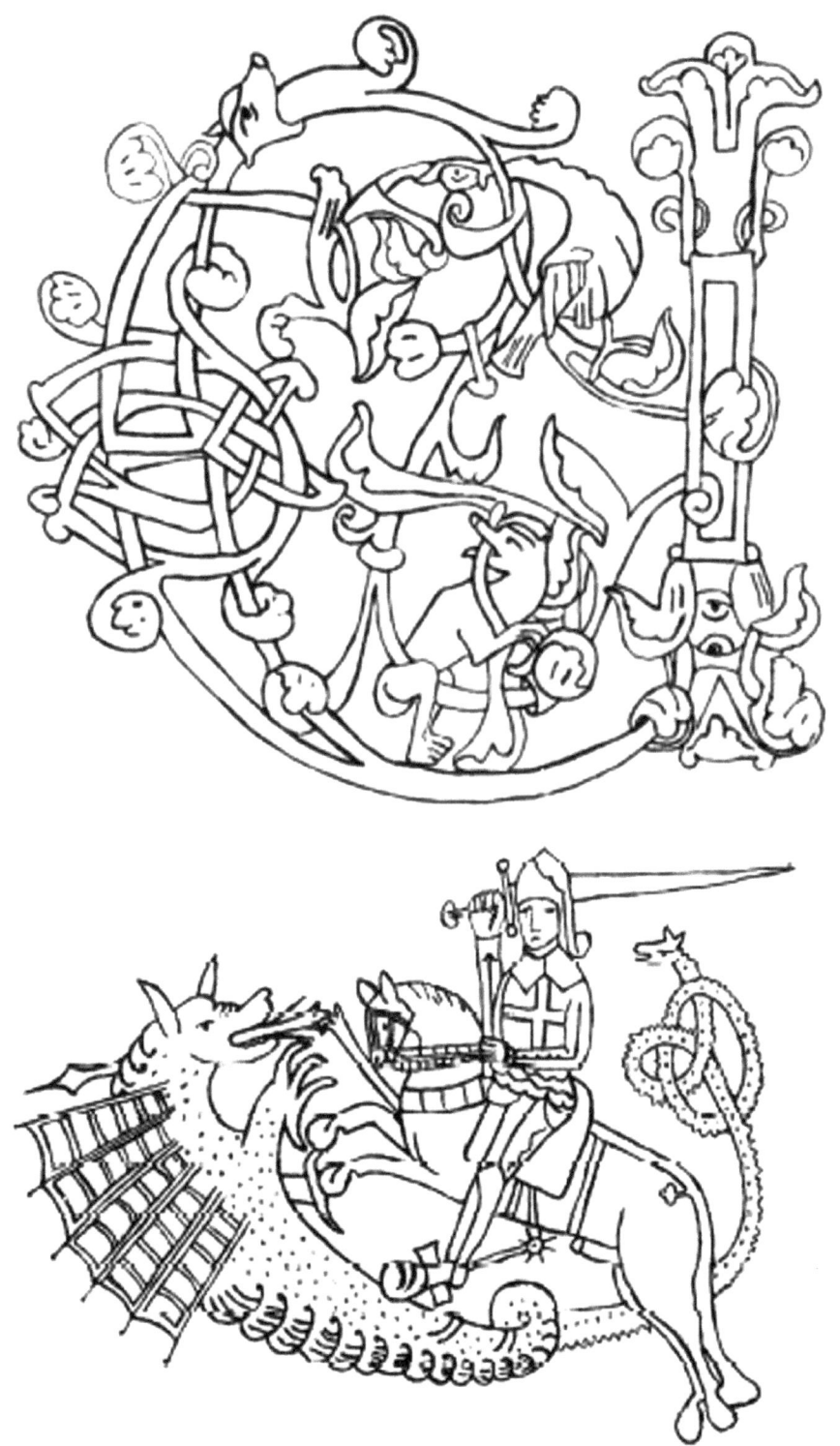

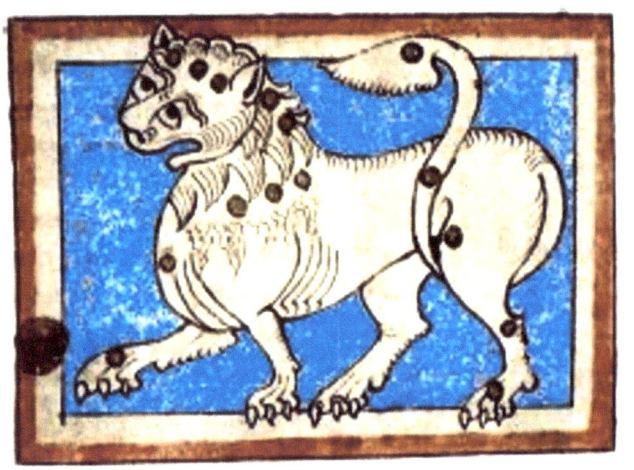

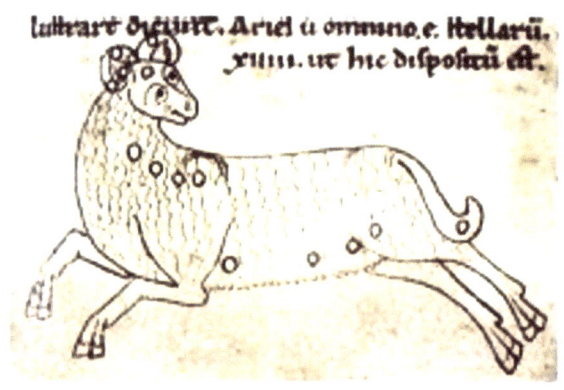

lustrare dic̅iiiii. Aries ū omnino. e̅. stellarū
xiiii. ut hic dispositū est.

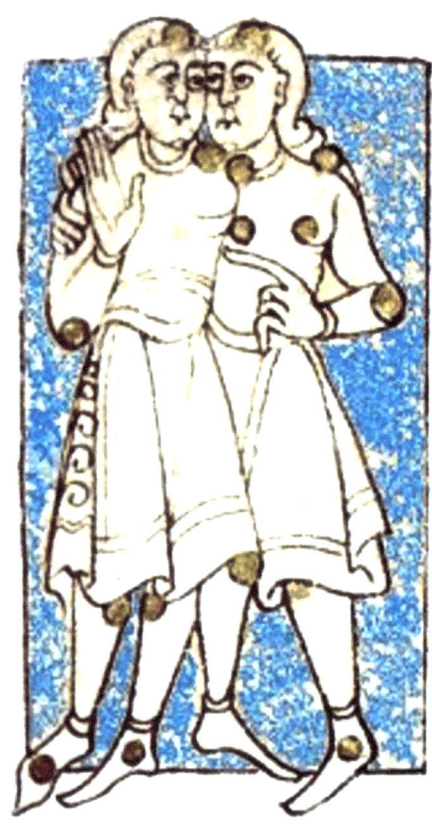

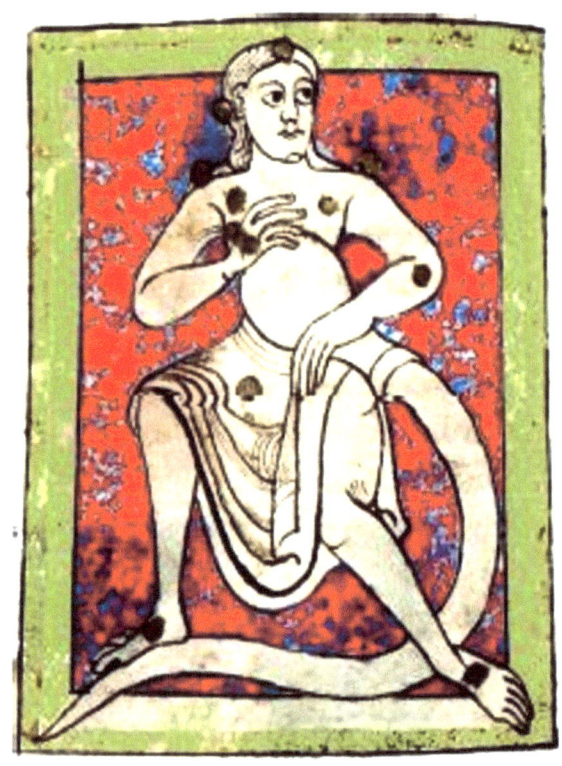

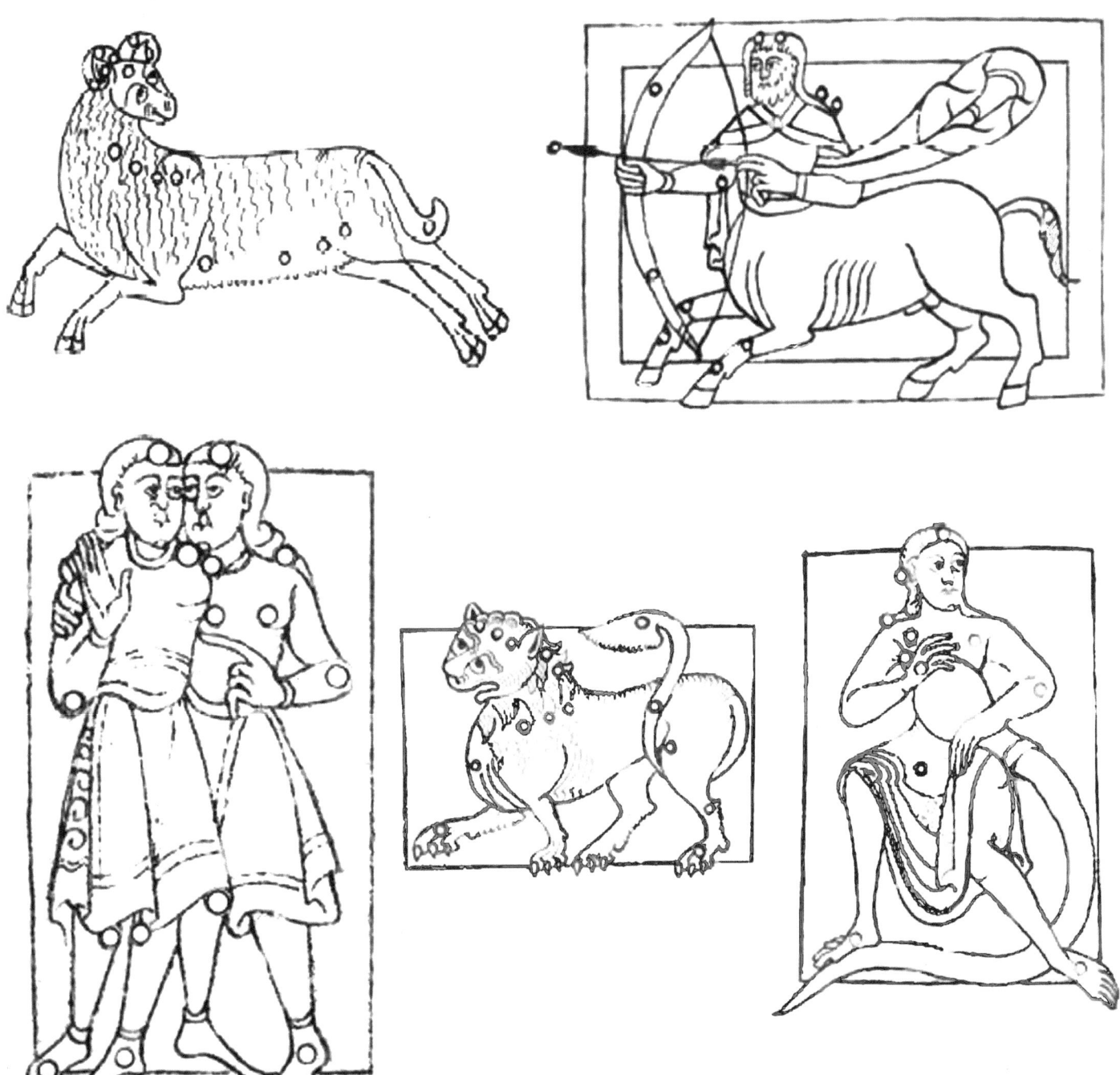

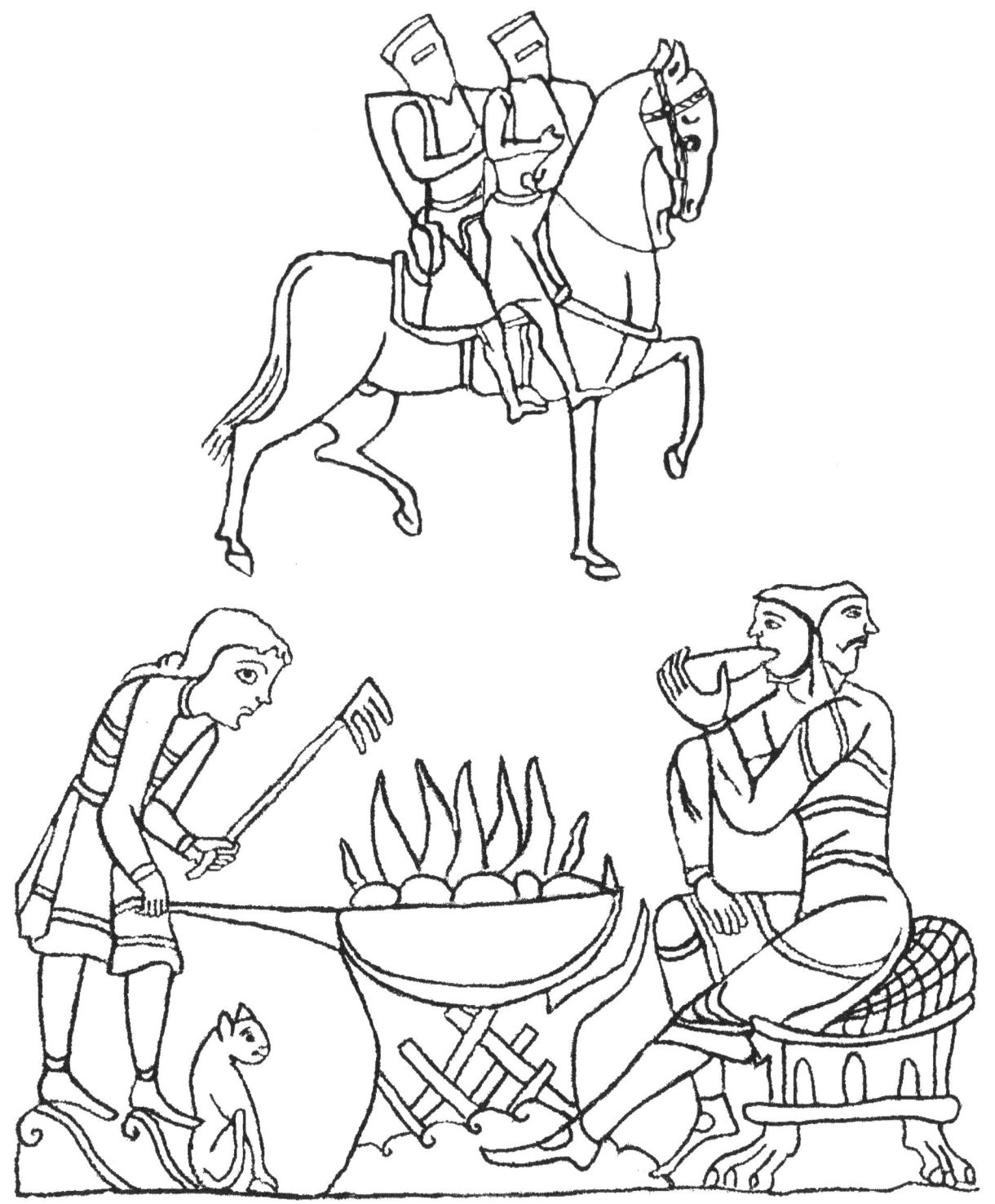

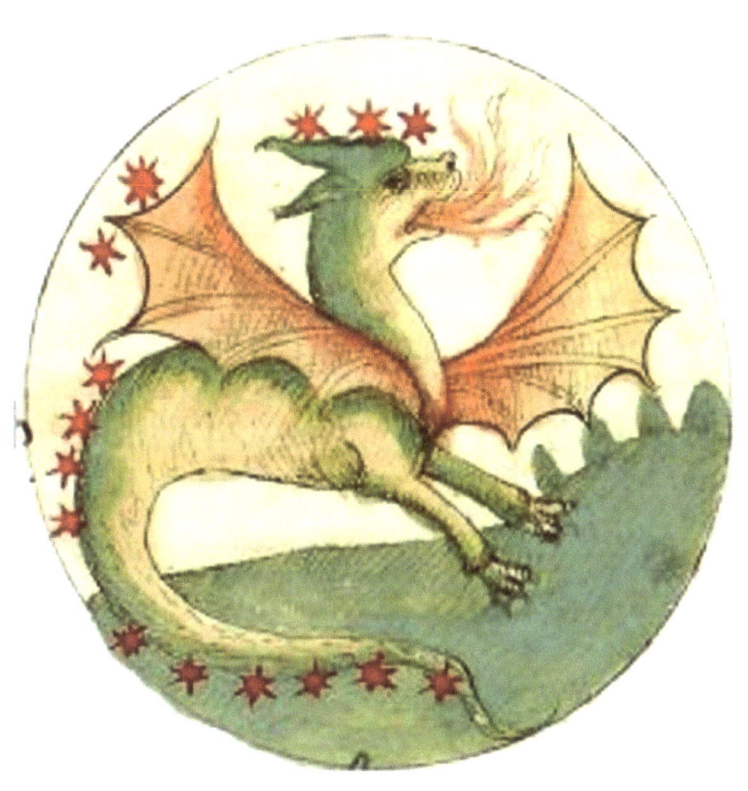

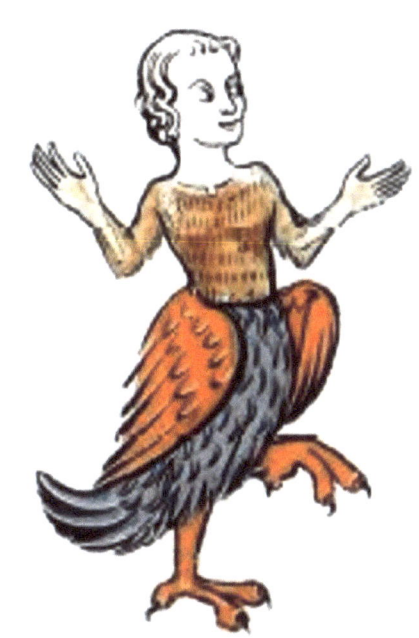

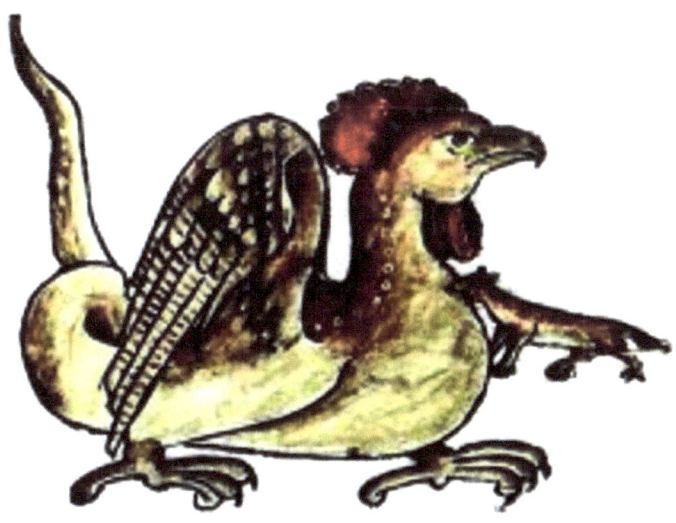

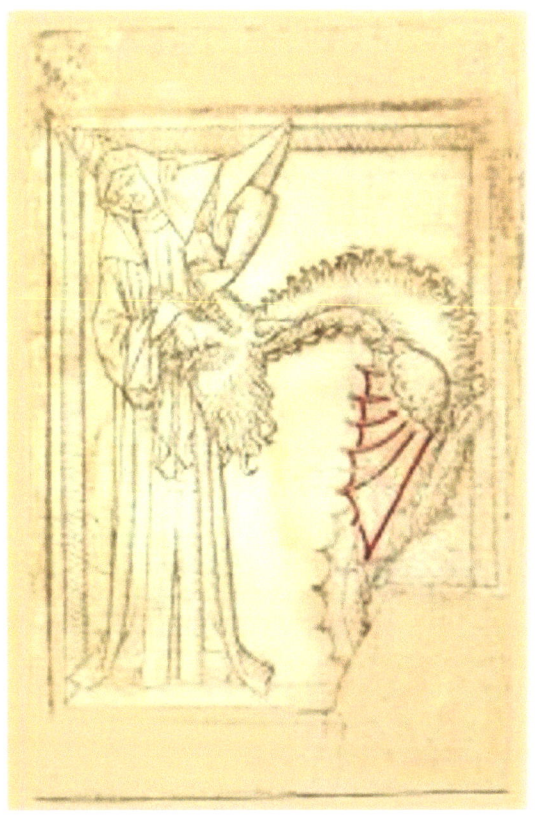

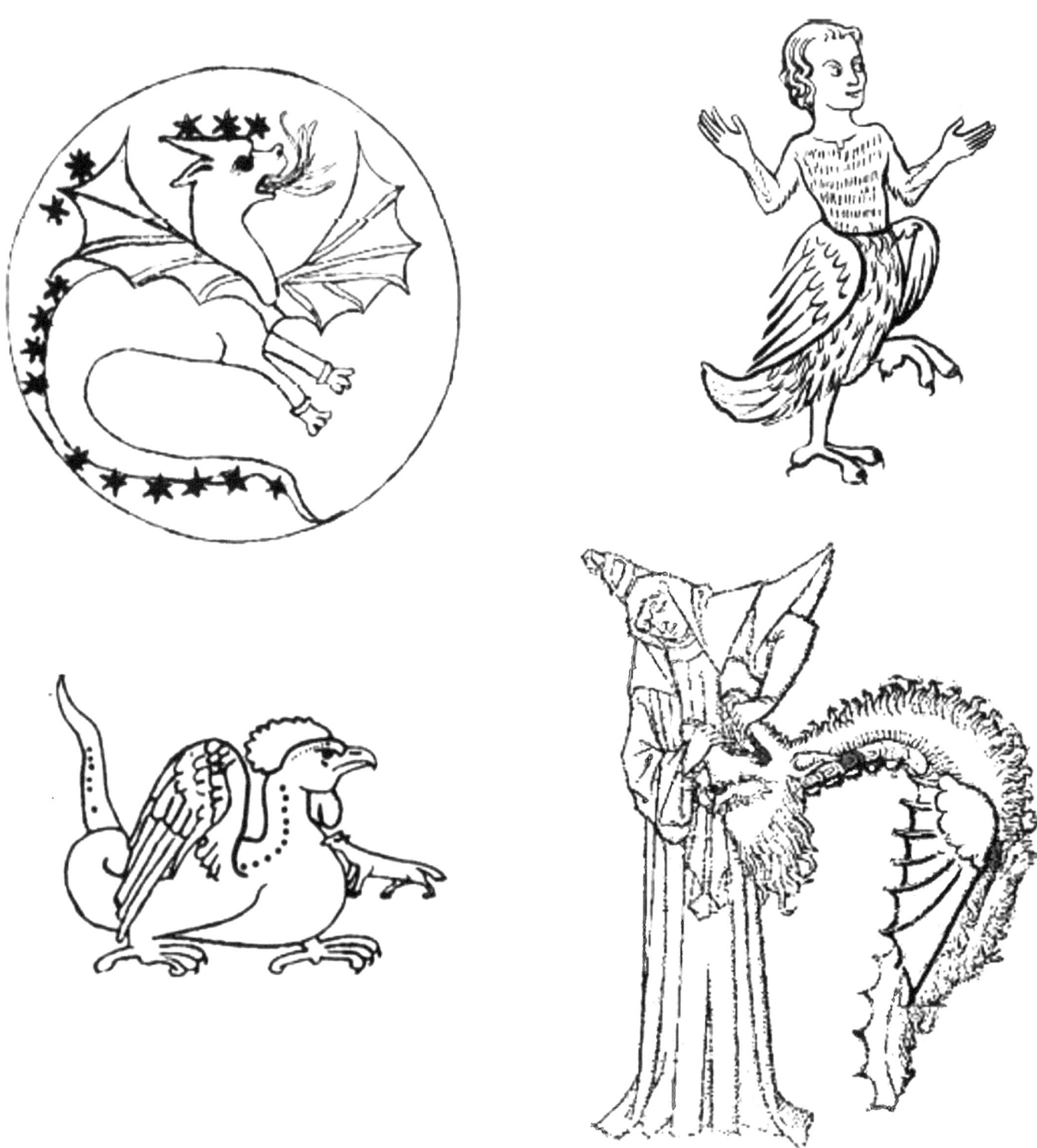

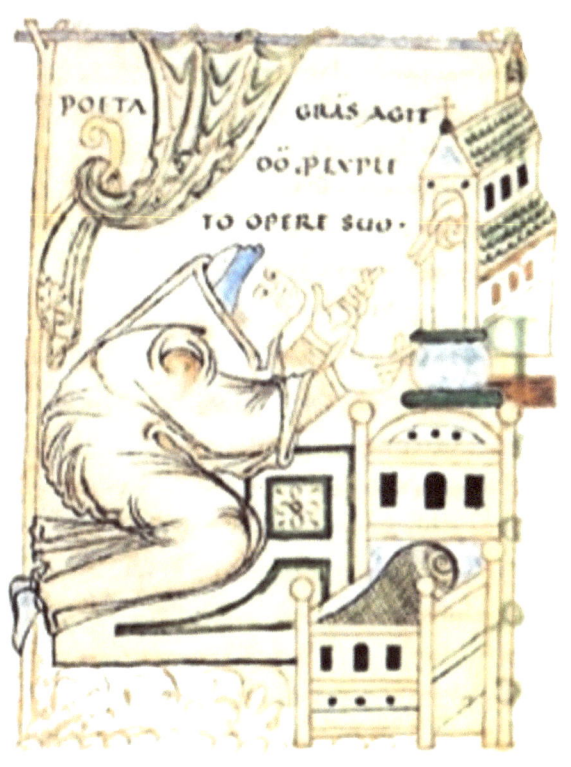

POETA GRĀS AGIT OŌ PLVPLI TO OPERE SVO.

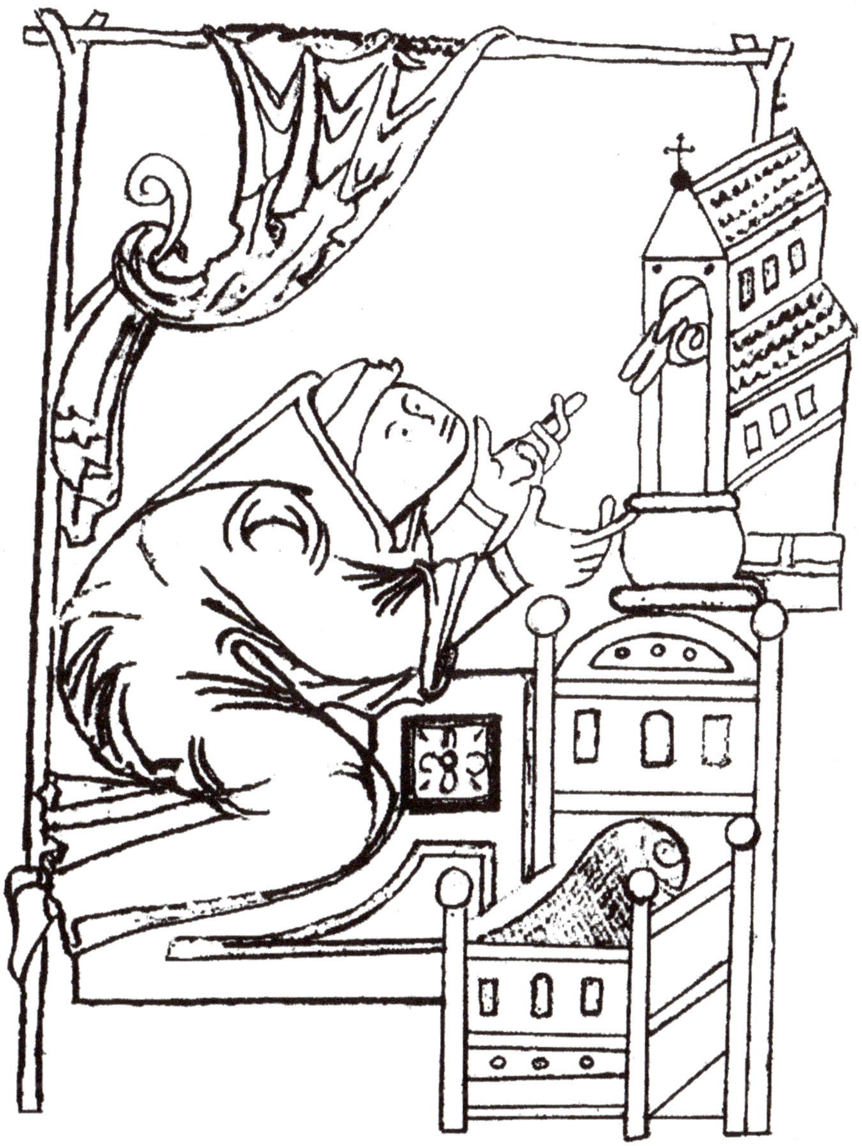

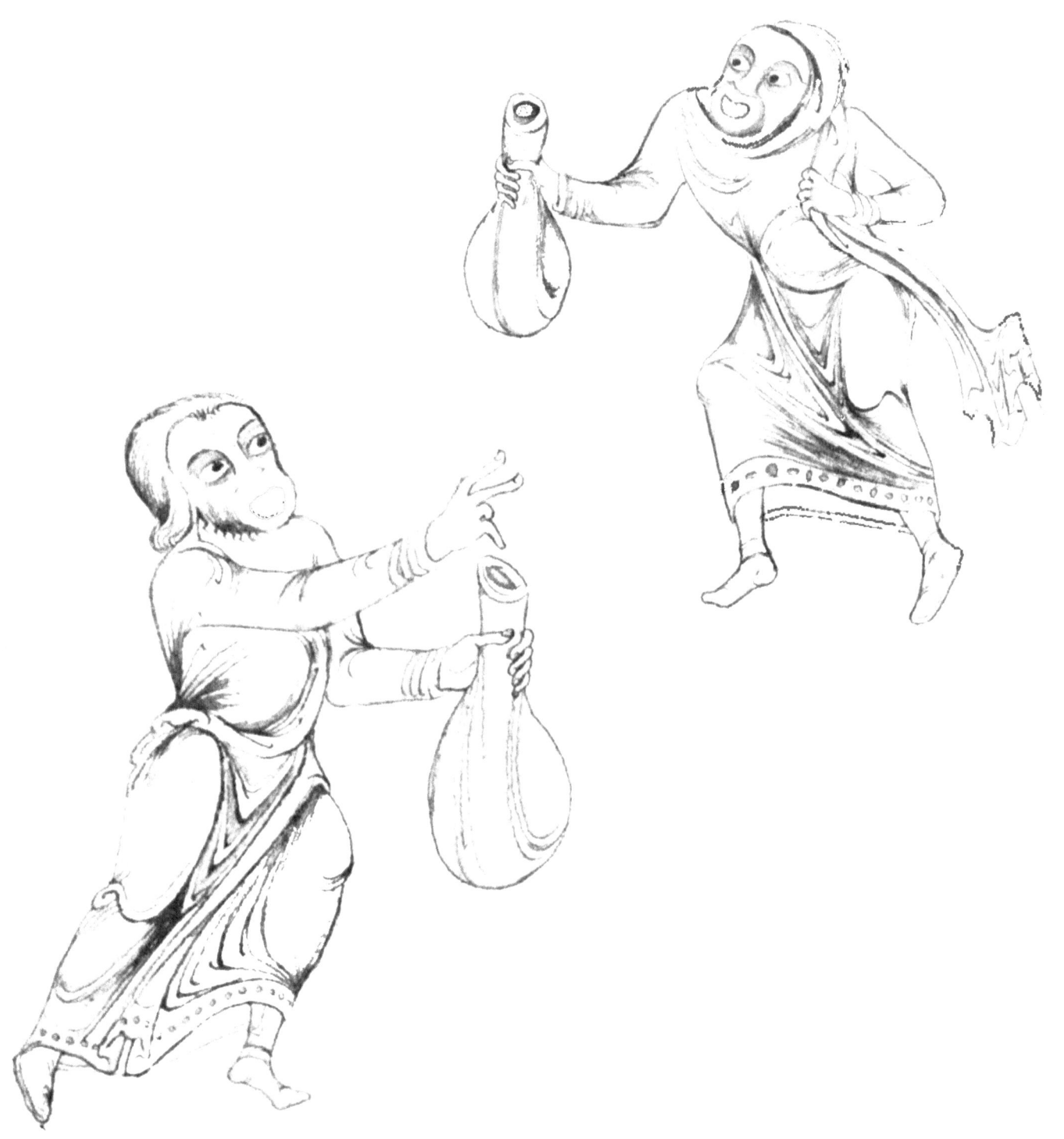

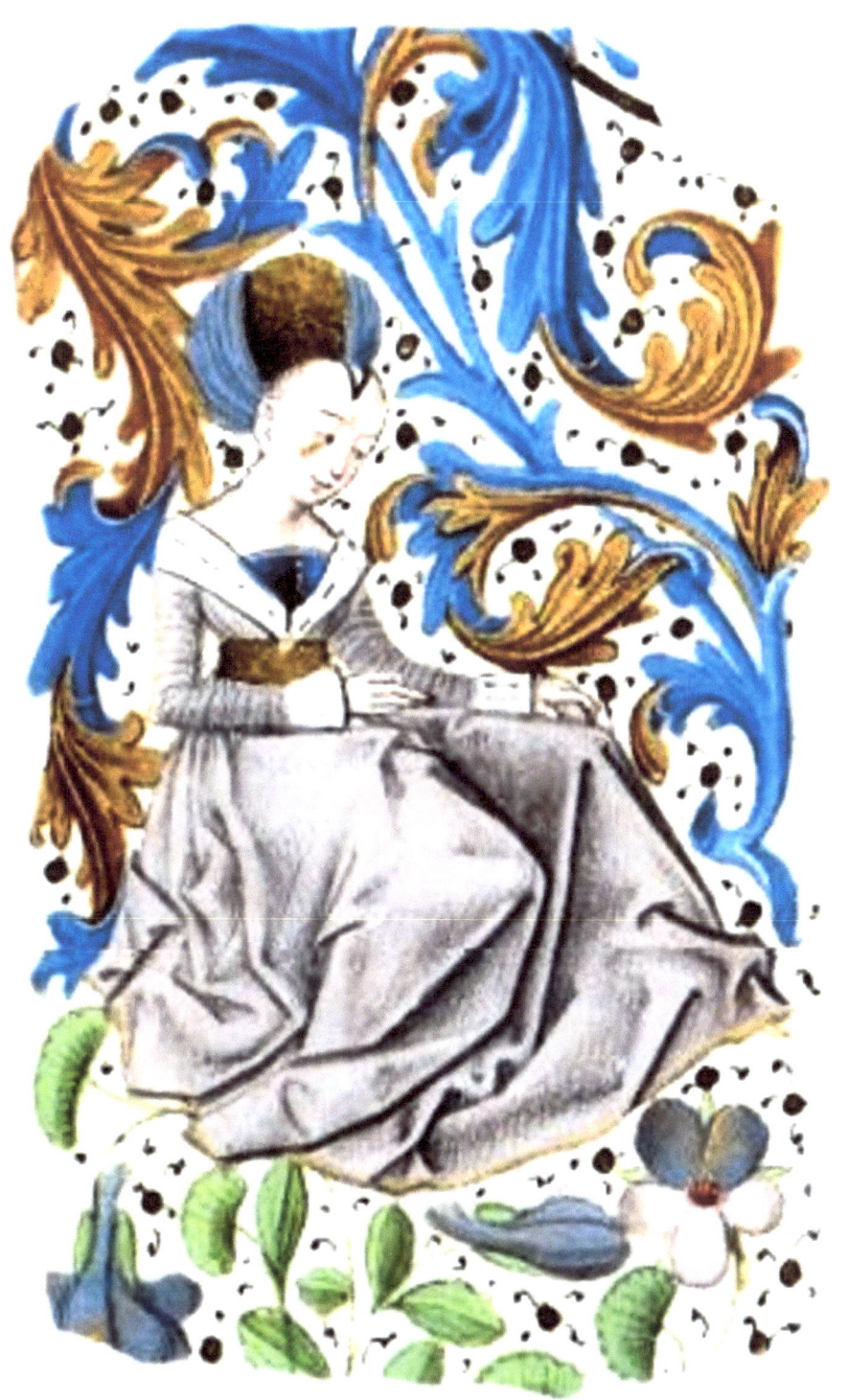

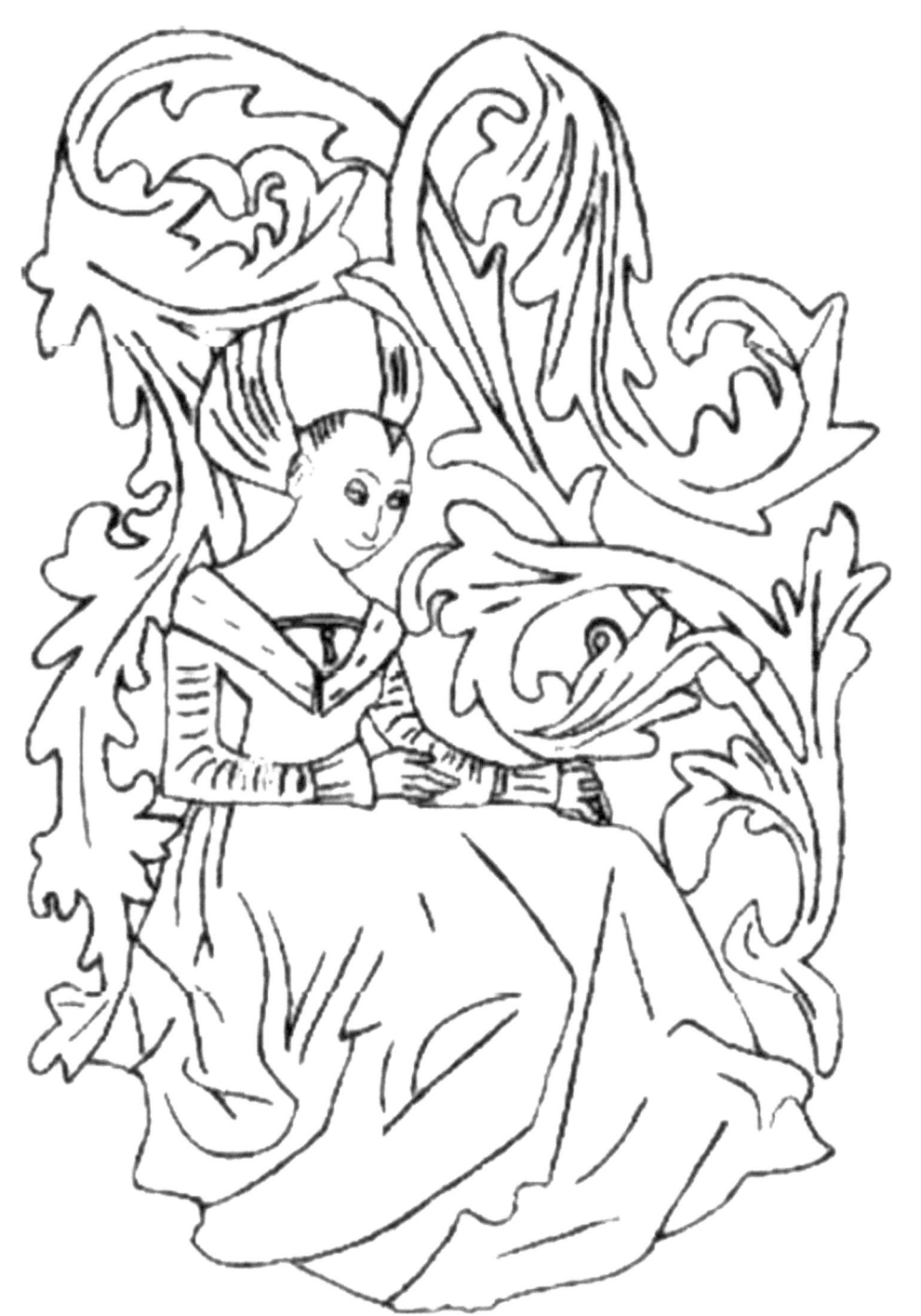

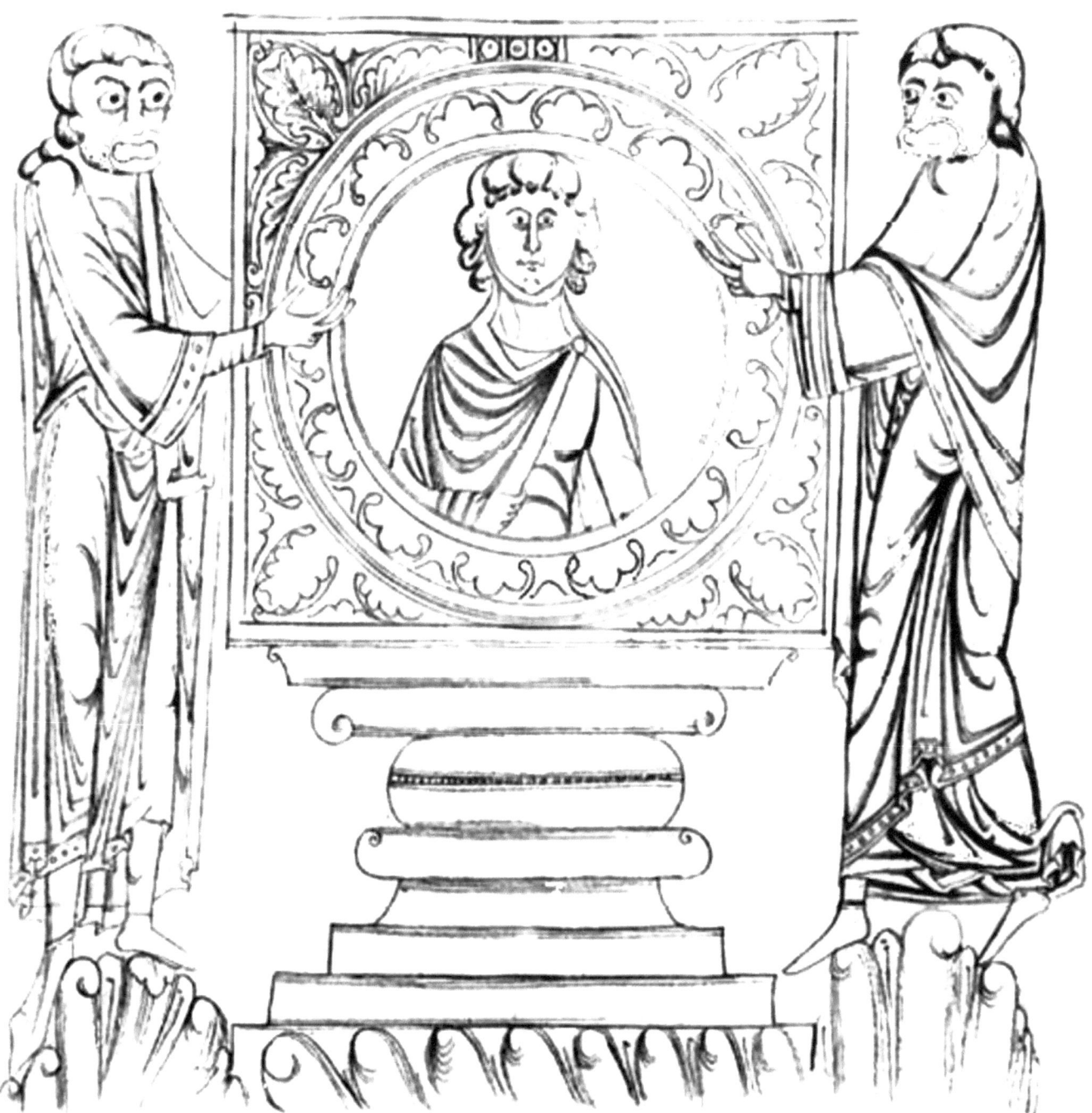

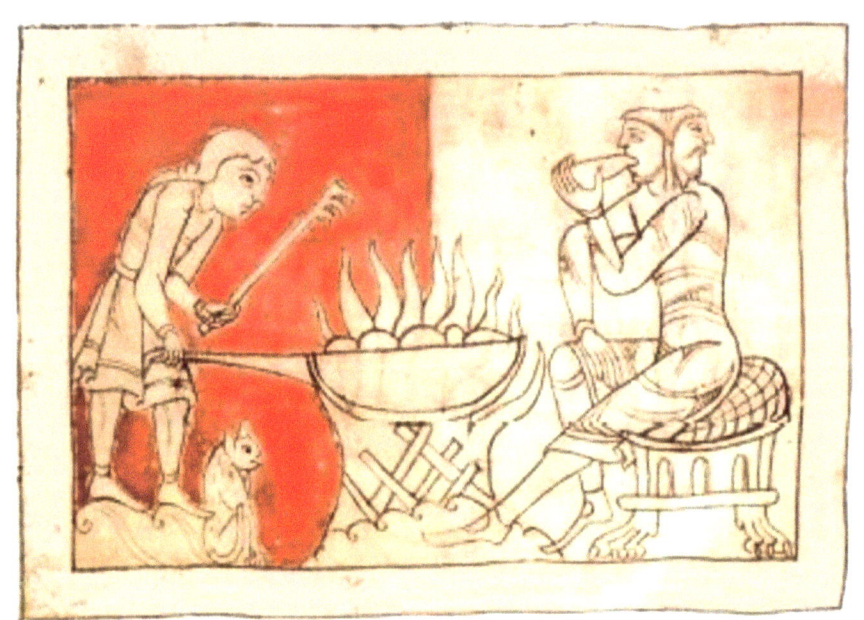

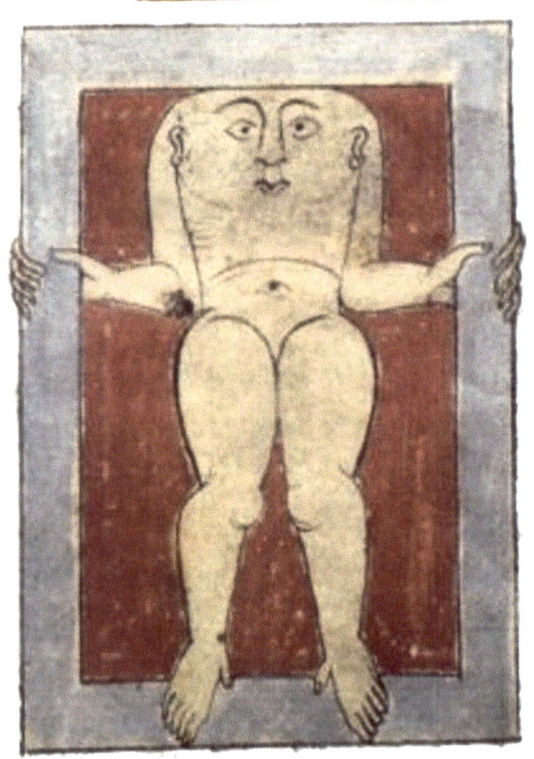

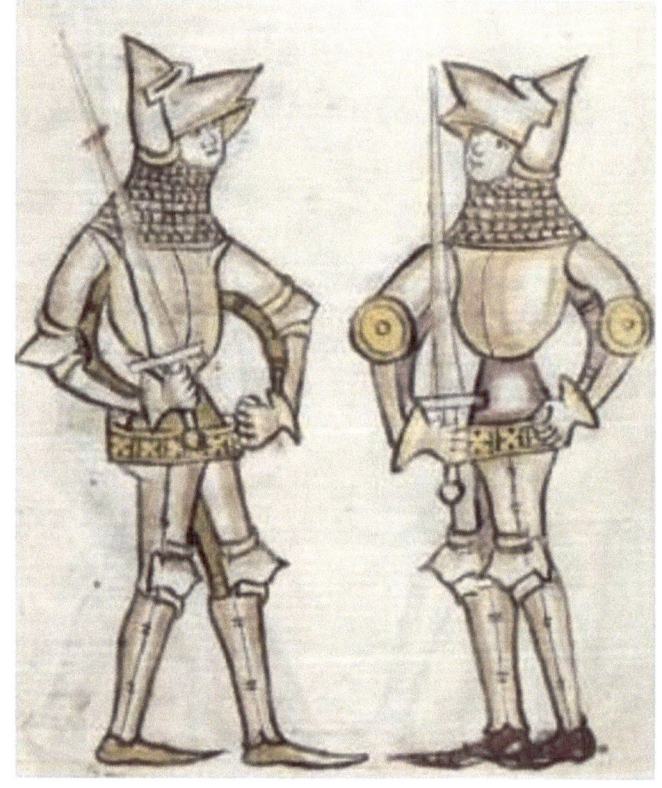

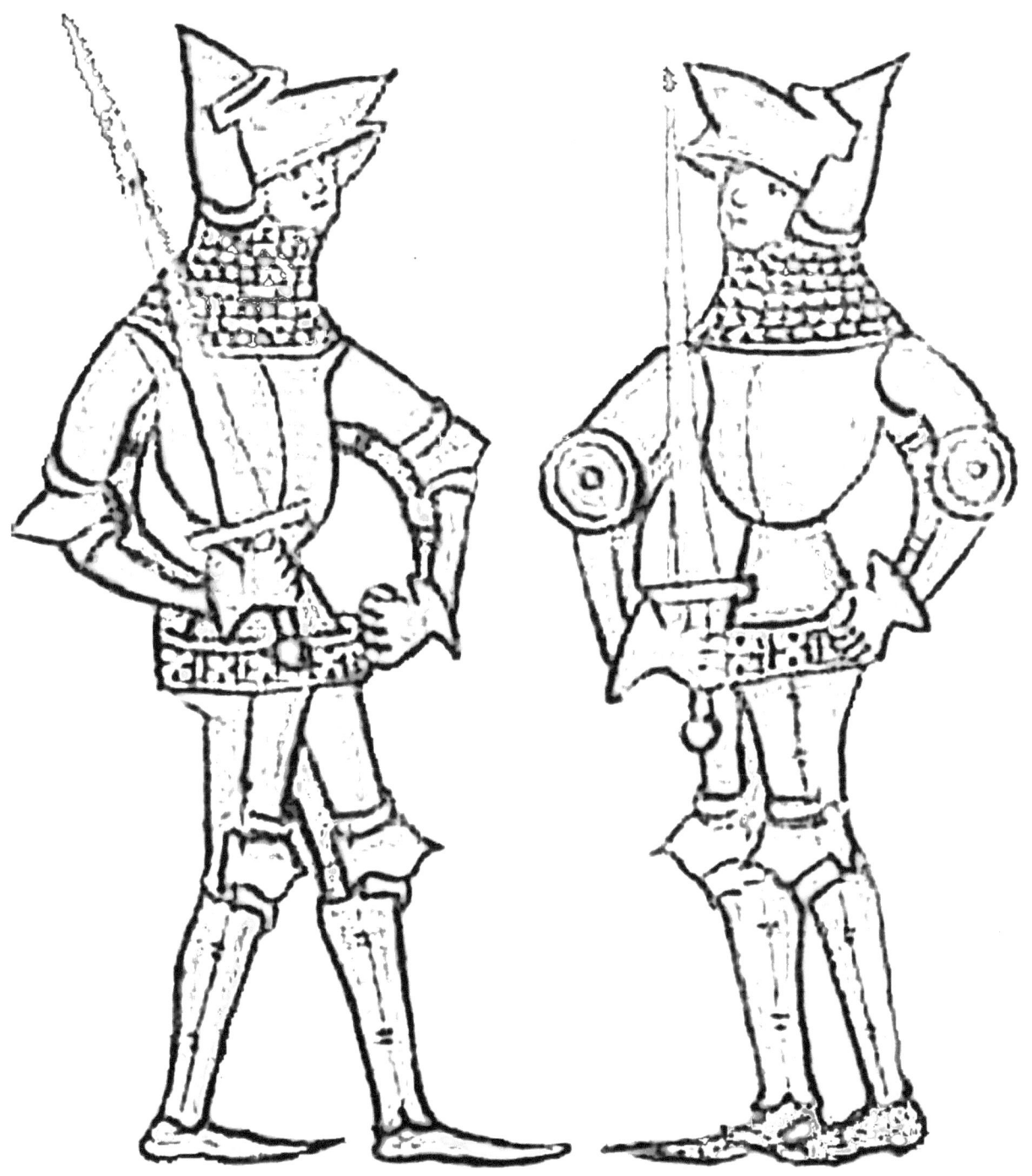

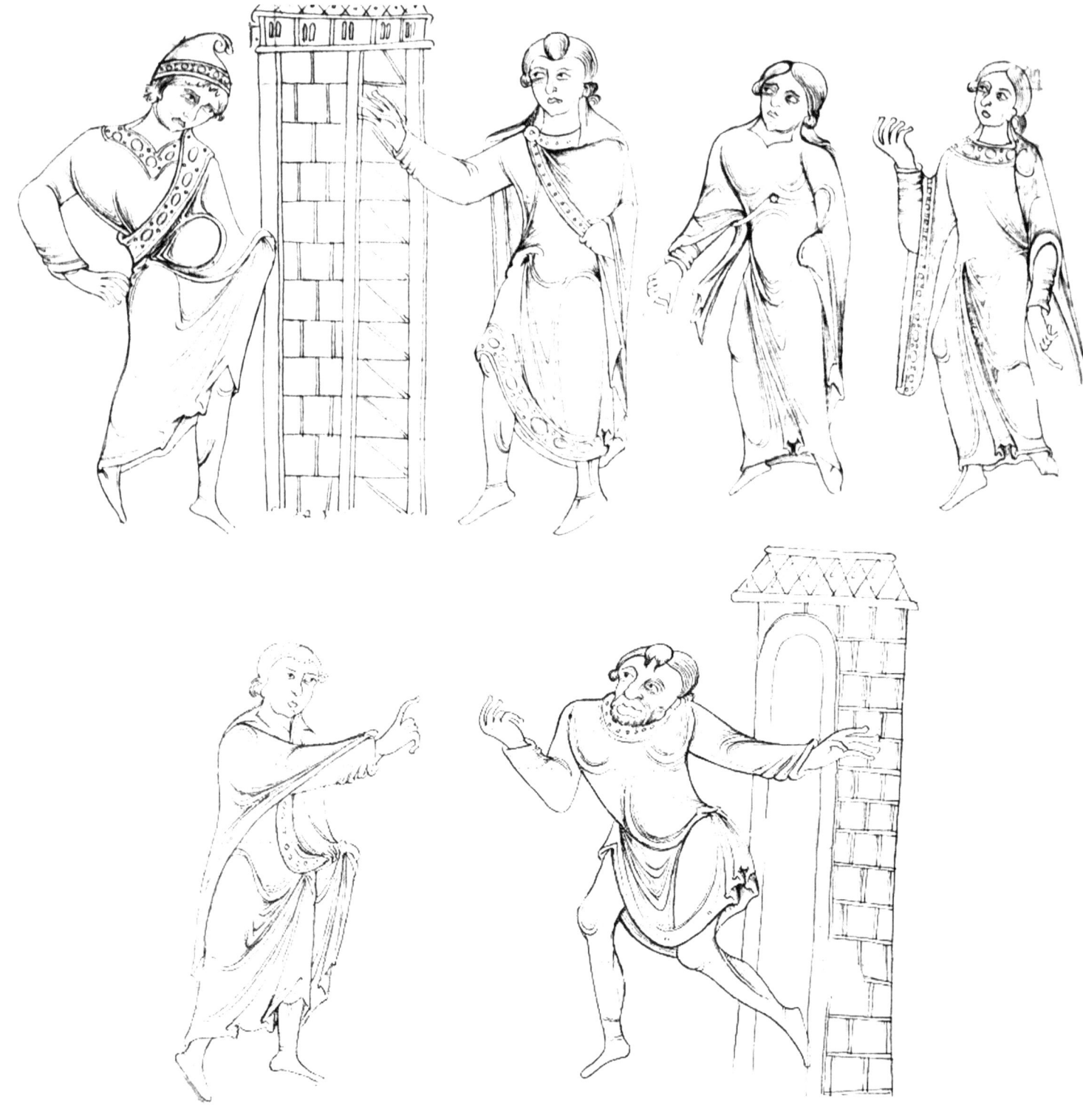

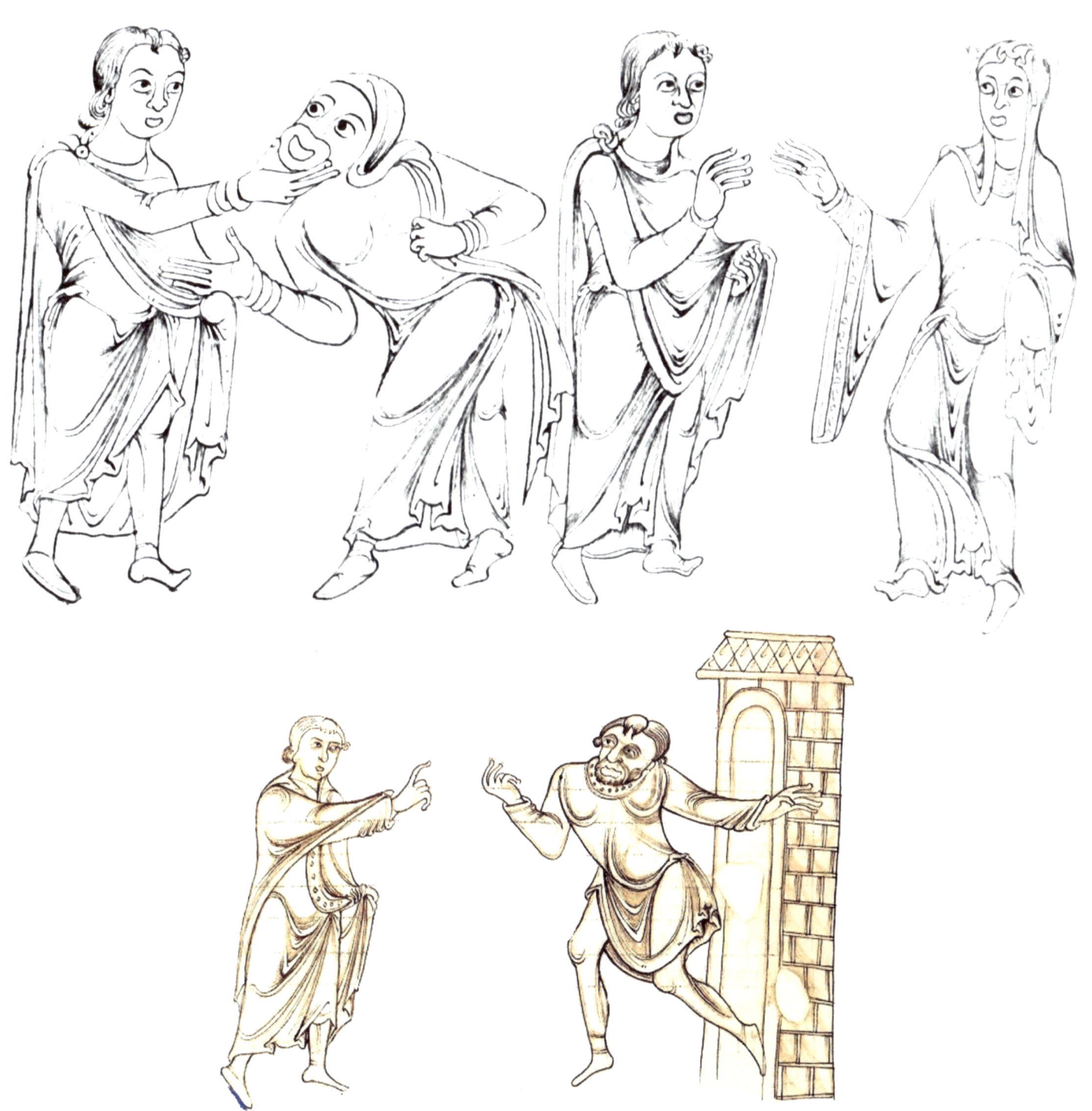

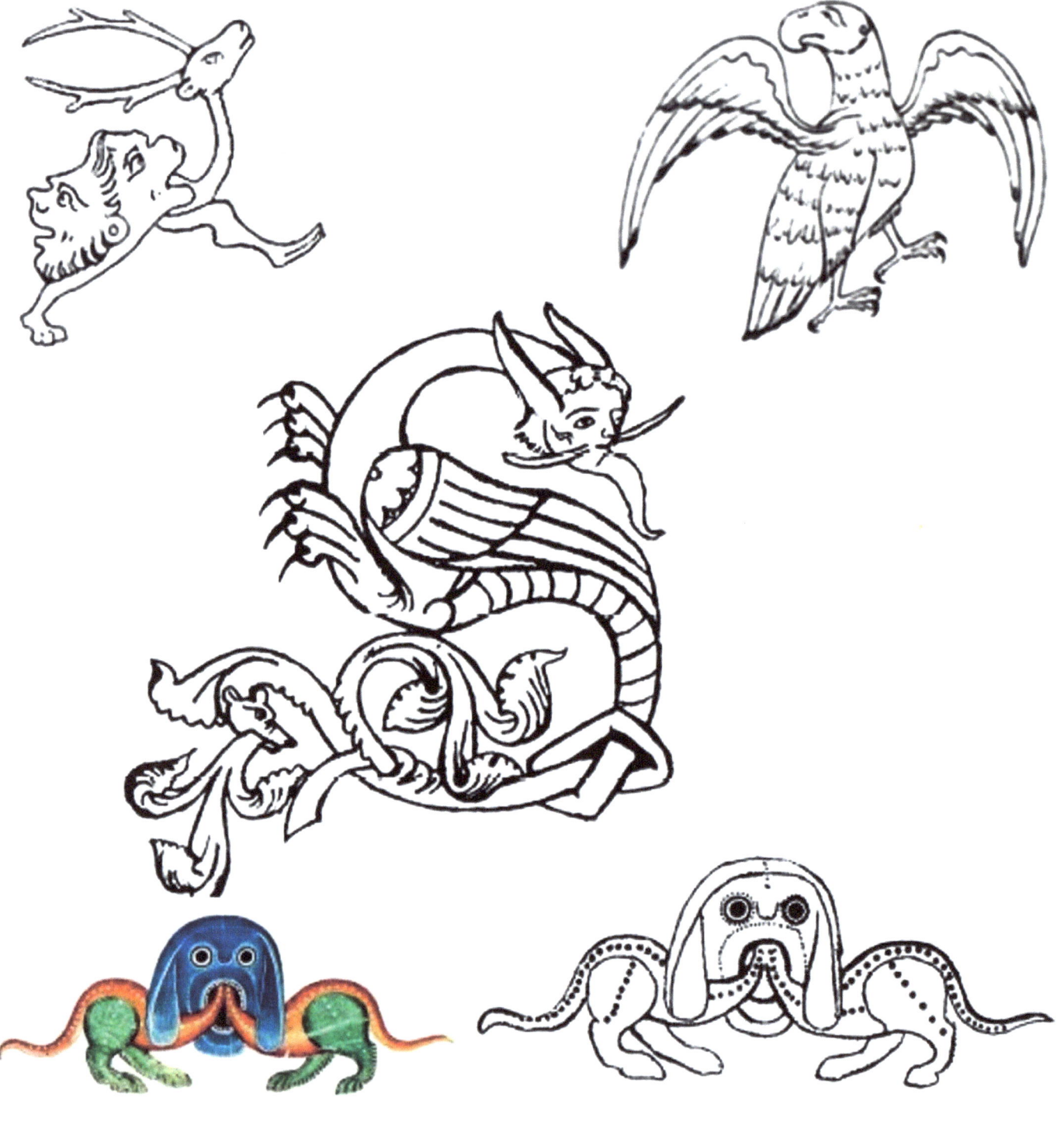

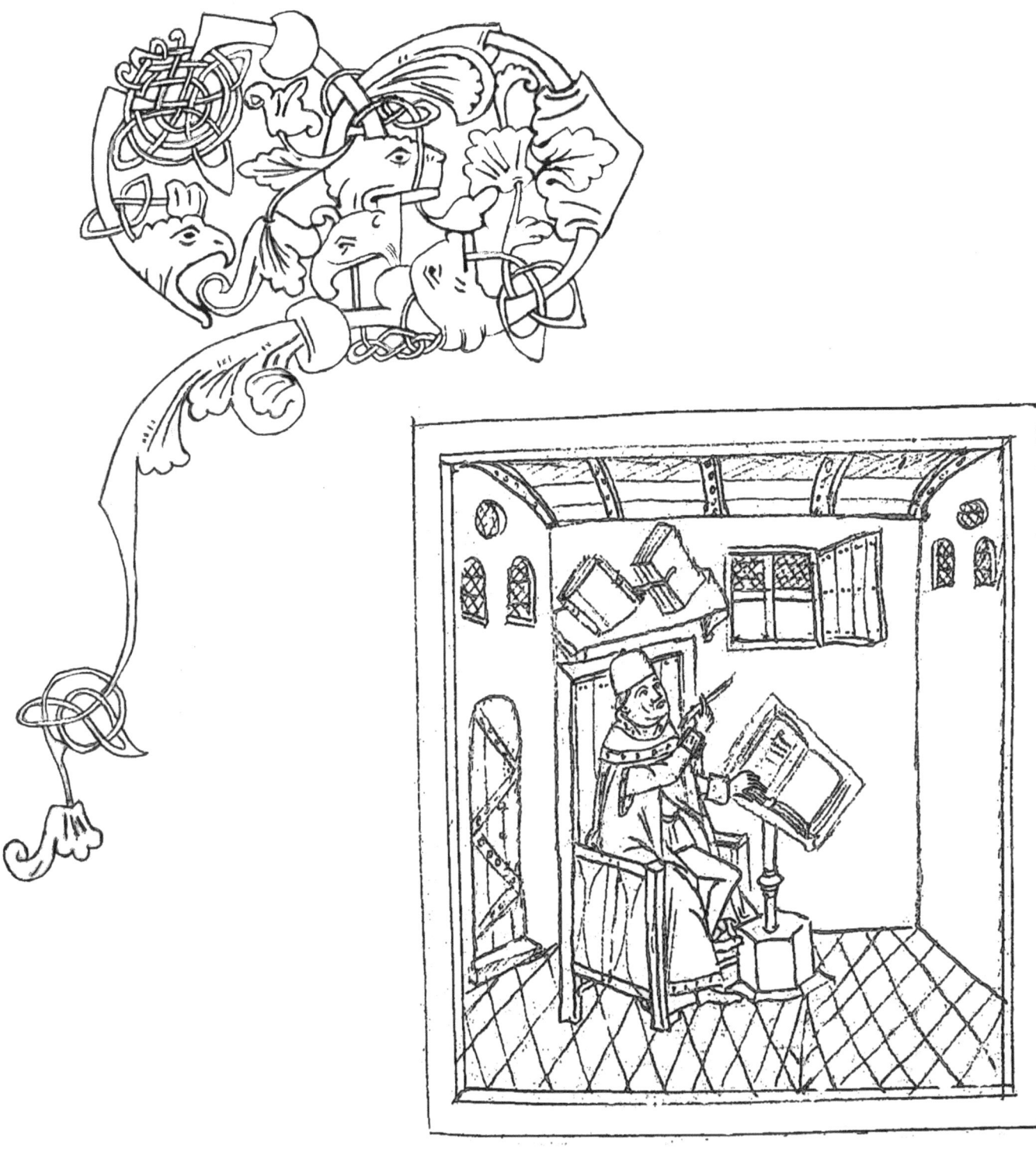

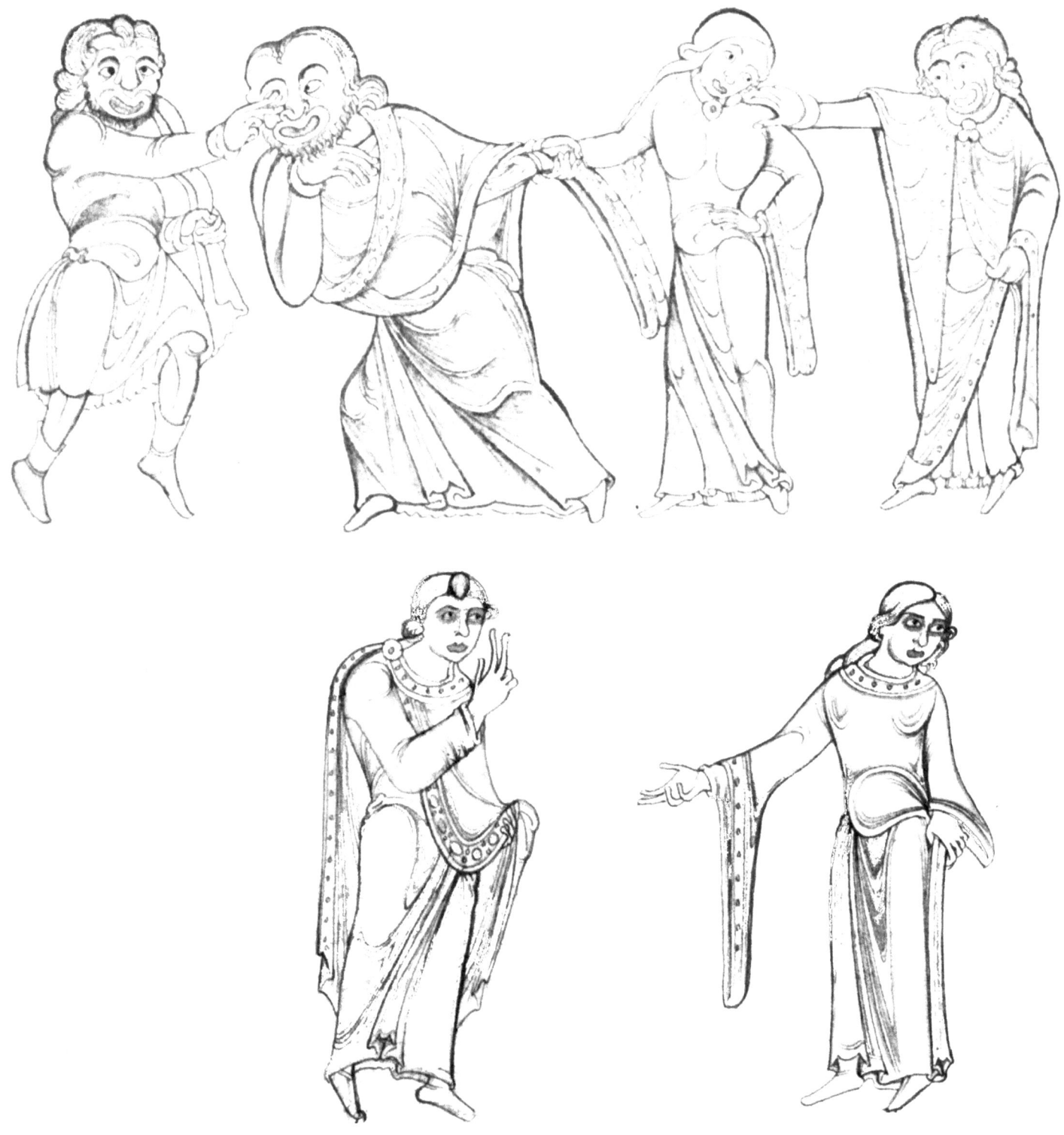

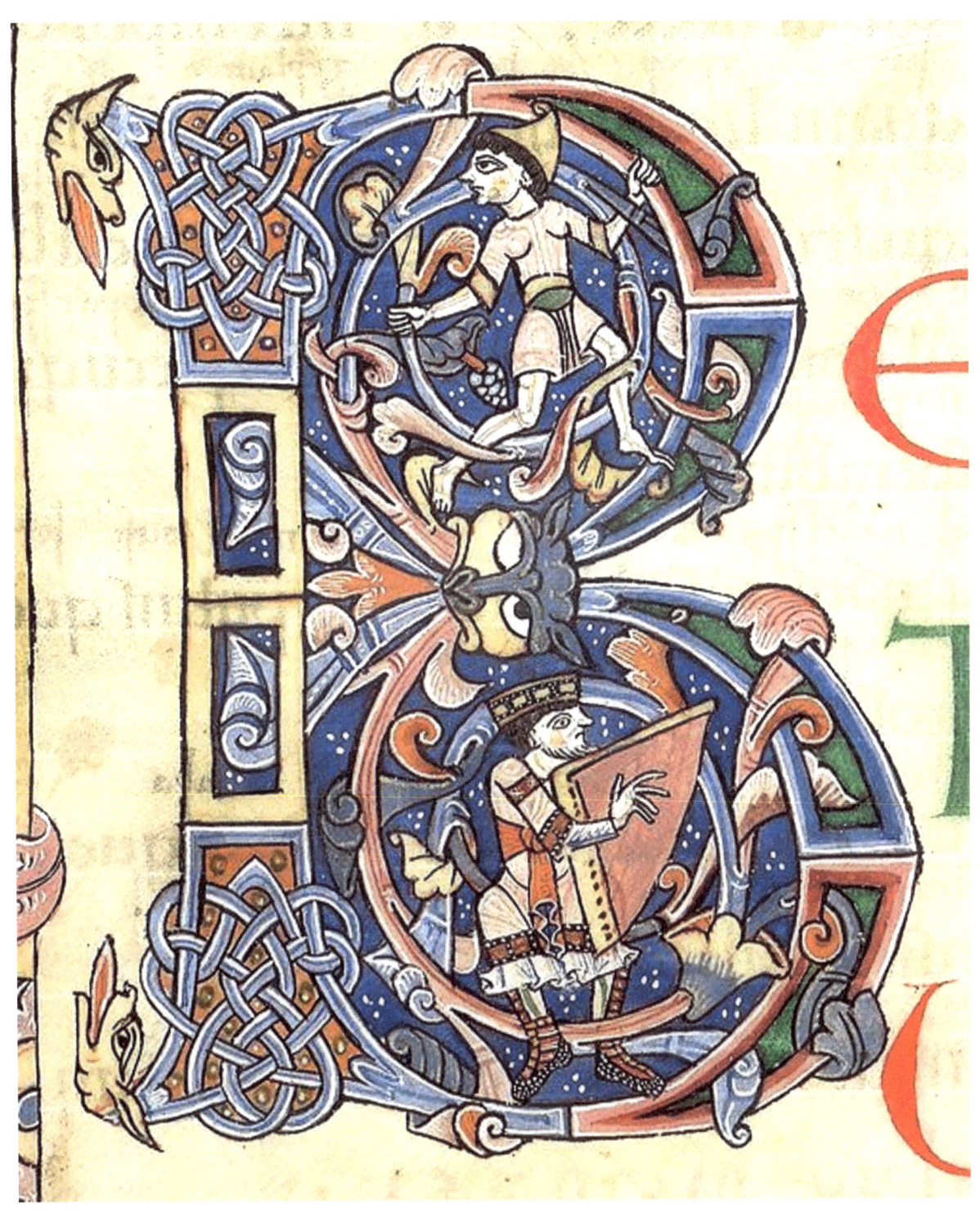

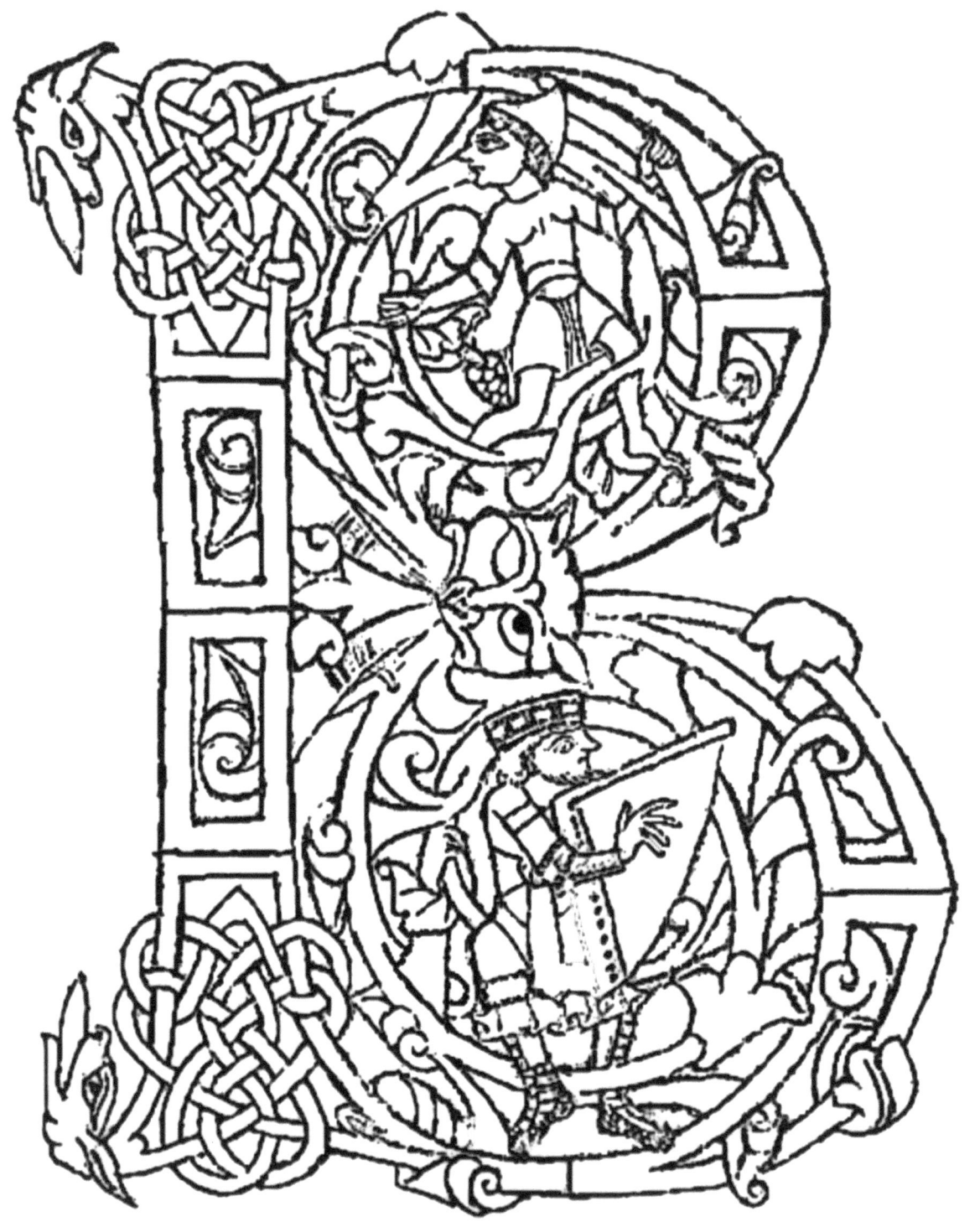

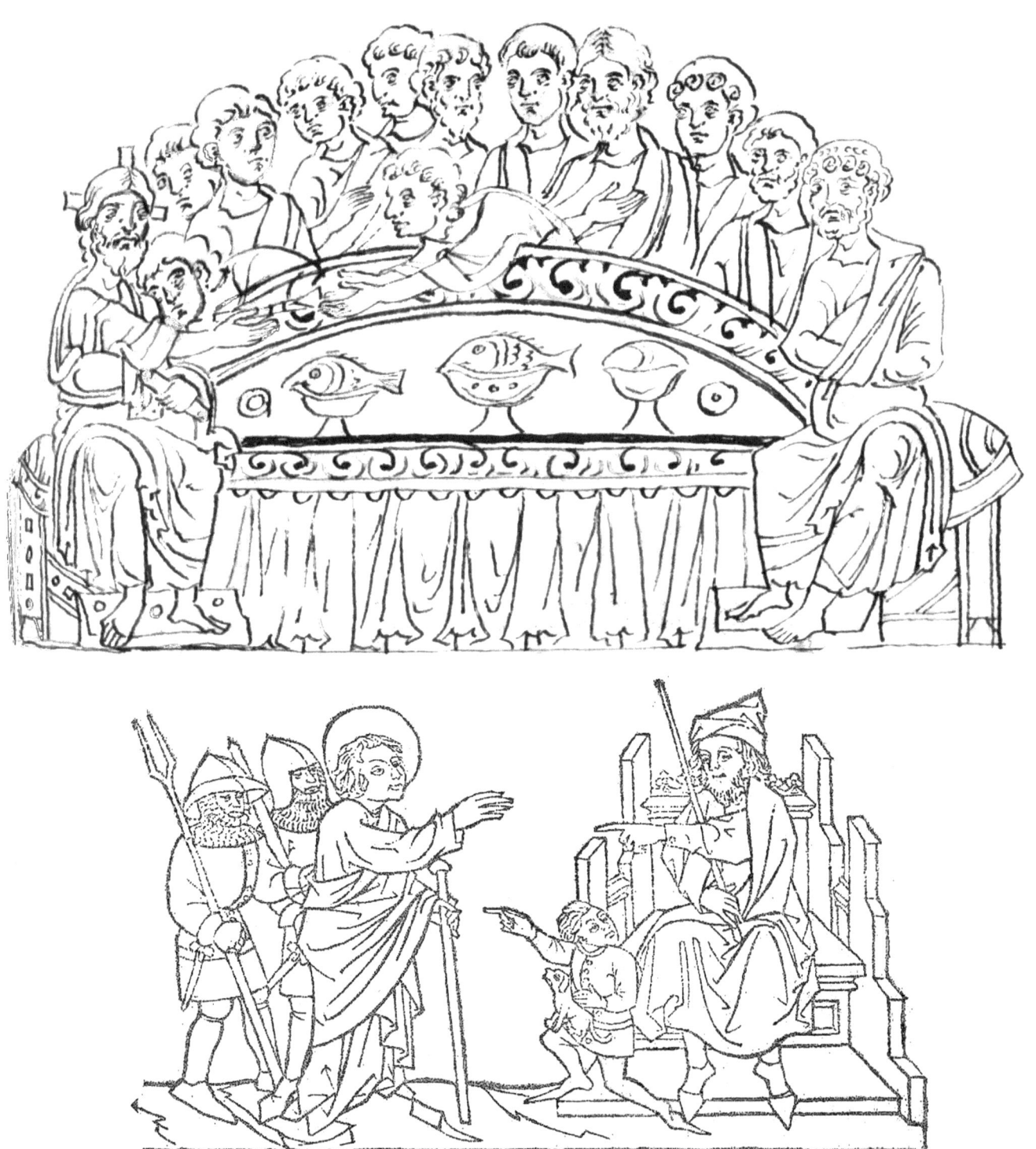

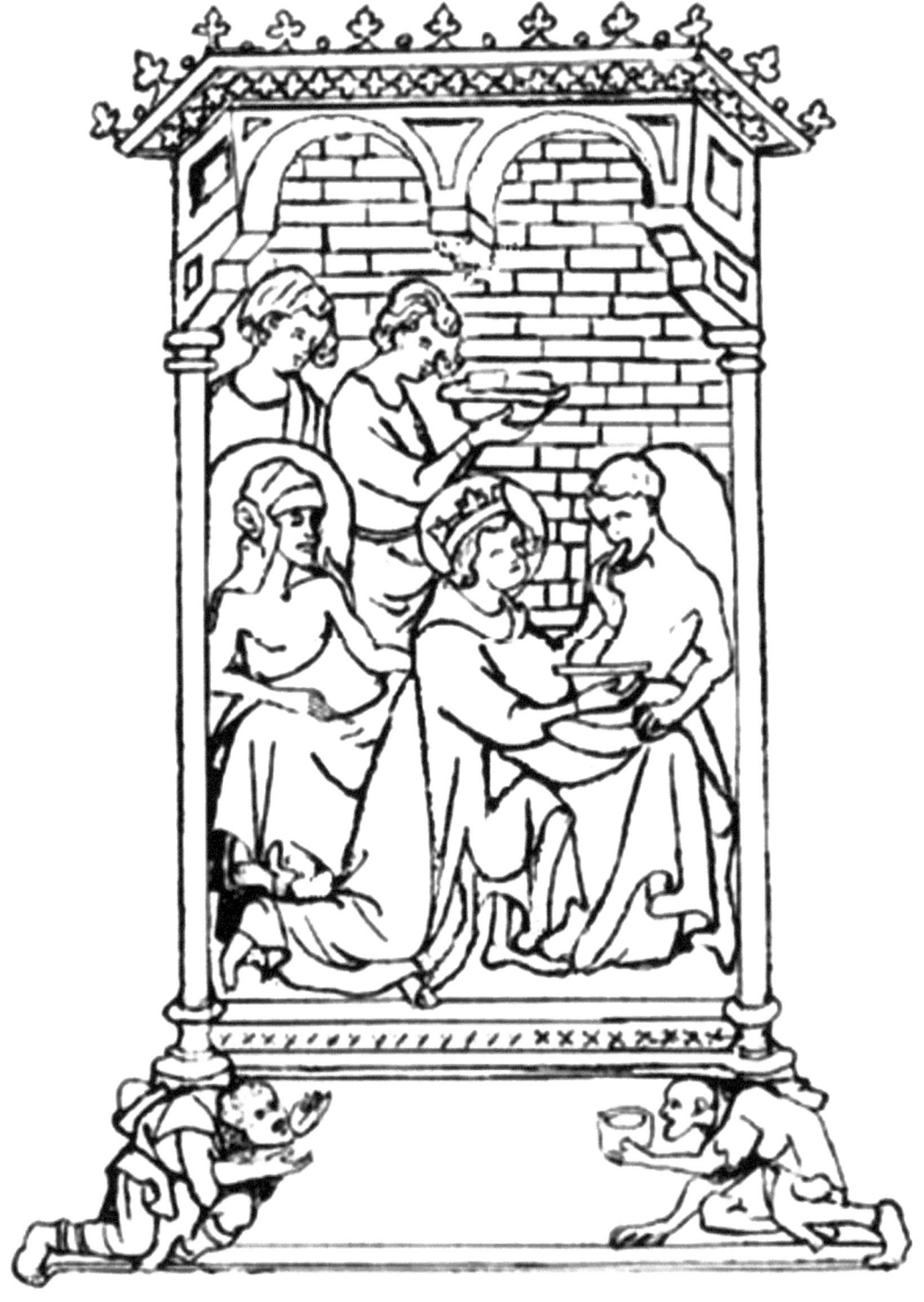

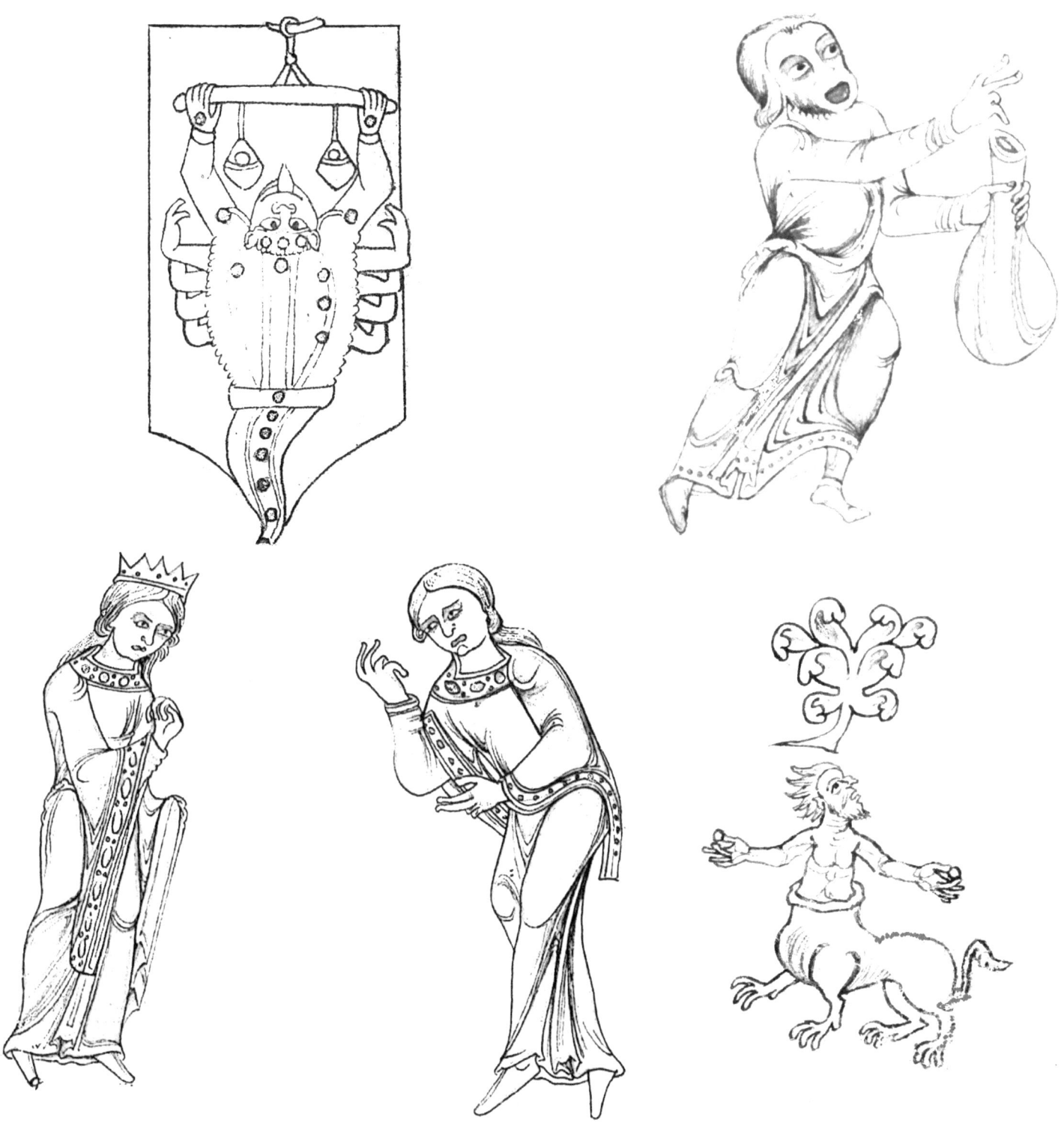

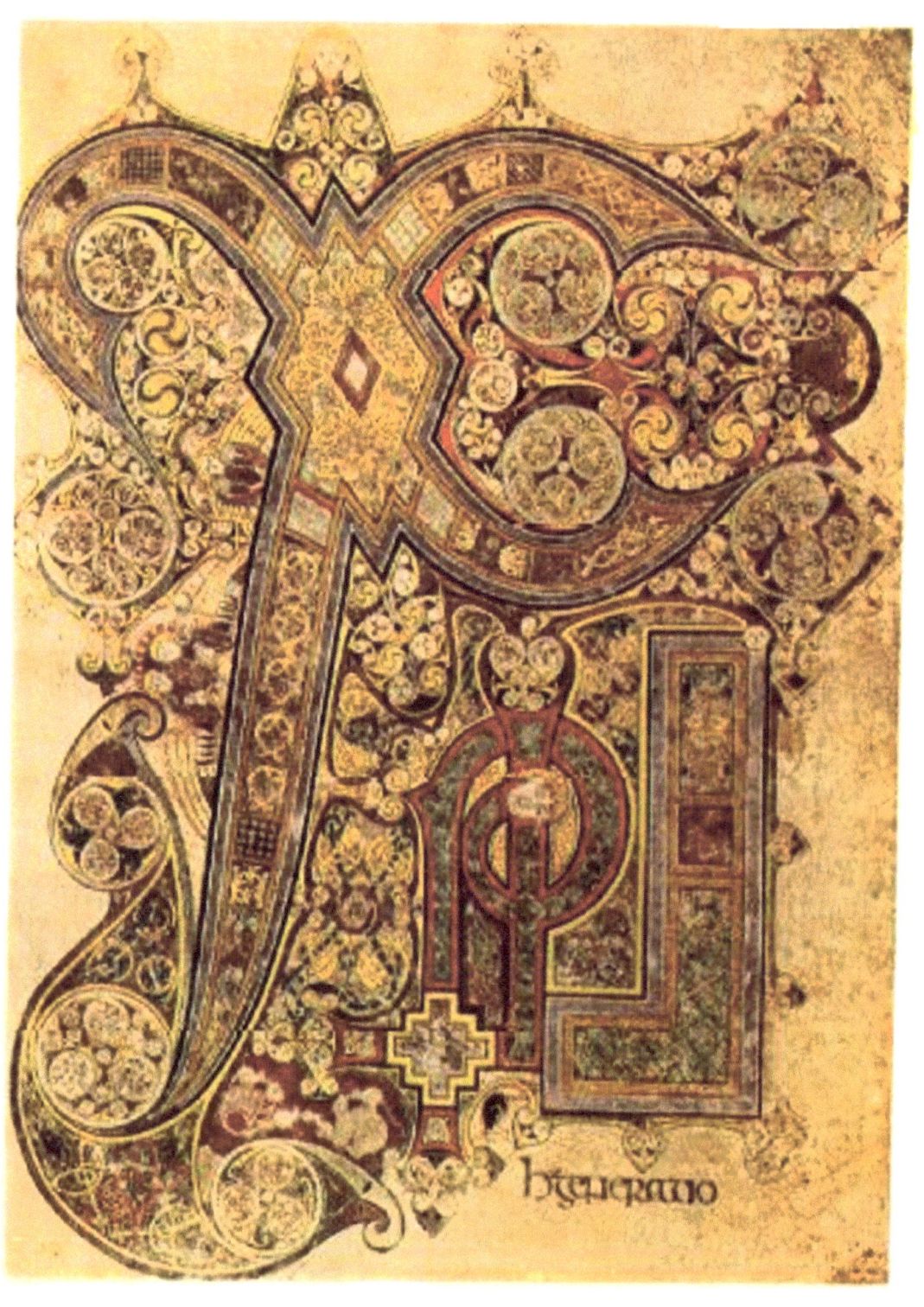

hgeneratio